D0529748

ICE CREAM & FRIENDS

FOOD52

ICE CREAM
& FRIENDS

60 RECIPES & RIFFS FOR SORBETS, SANDWICHES, NO-CHURN ICE CREAMS AND MORE

Editors of Food52

Photography by James Ransom

TEN SPEED PRESS
California | New York

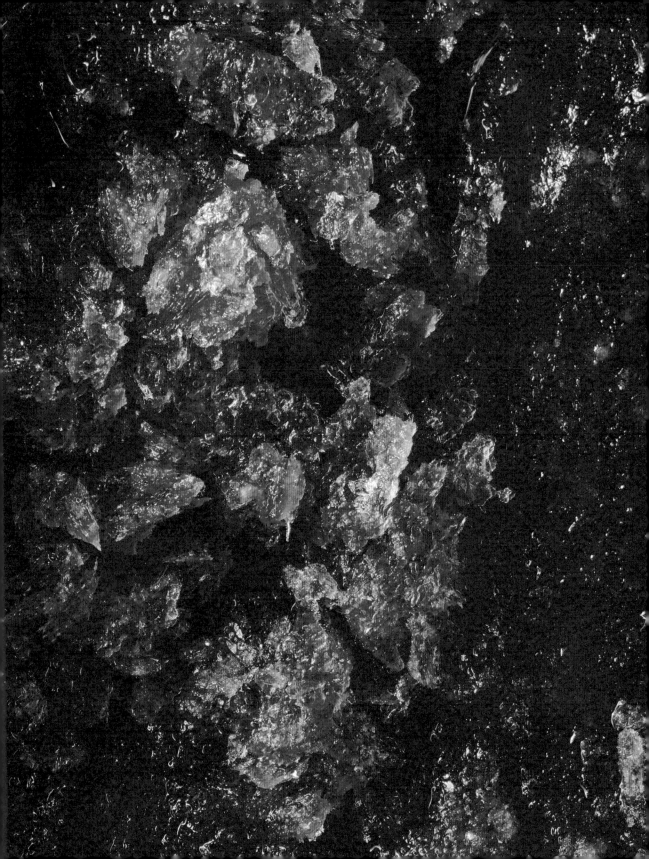

Contents

Foreword

Semifreddo is no more ice cream than a brownie is a cookie. The same could be said for gelato, custard, sherbet, milkshakes, fudgesicles, and paletas. This is why we called this book *Ice Cream & Friends*, because in our world, ice cream has lots of chilled pals and affable toppings, and we love them all.

We were tired of books that made ice cream so *serious* and so *difficult*. Or that made readers feel inadequate for not owning an ice cream maker. We wanted a book that made it clear that frozen desserts don't have to be a special-occasion endeavor, but something that's much easier to whip up than most cakes. We've included no-churn recipes aplenty (page 48) and tips for making store-bought ice cream more interesting (pages 26, 29, and 63). And there are a billion add-on ideas, give or take a few. You will learn how to make sprinkles (page 4)!

And for those who have mastered ice cream, we give you new challenges in Philadelphia-style ice cream (page 16), frozen custard (page 117), and ice milk (page 153). We show you how to make velvet (page 78) and spoom (page 75). And we've loaded this handy book with genius tips, riffs, and mini recipes that we hope will inspire you to dream up your own creations.

Many of the flavors in these recipes are nostalgic (yet surprising). Black walnuts are candied in hot honey (page 42). Saltines form the bookends for a brownie ice cream sandwich (page 33). Others charge forward, like a gelato with avocado (page 154). We fell in love with savory tomato, peach, and basil sorbet (page 147).

But perhaps our most beloved ice cream friend of all is Burnt Toast Ice Cream (page 148). Although the two of us are very experienced cooks, we burn toast. All. The. Time. Our toast mishaps were so frequent that we originally named our company Burnt Toast (Food52 won out over time). As we recently discovered, there's no longer a need to scrape the char from our singed bread or throw it away. Next time, save it for a batch of ice cream that will embrace the toast's accidental condition and transform it into something addictive and delightful.

We hope that you, too, will make friends with this book and fill your freezer until it's bursting!

—Amanda Hesser & Merrill Stubbs, founders of Food52

Introduction

None of us editors at Food52 run an ice cream shop. We don't have professional-grade ice cream makers or freezers. We are not named Ben or Jerry, but, like you, we adore ice cream. And while we happily eat ice cream from the store, we know that ice cream made at home is better—its consistency pillowy, its flavor pronounced, its style up to us.

In the pages that follow, you'll find recipes for ice cream, sure—they range from the best versions of classics to the strange yet good—but you'll also find sorbet, sherbet, slushies, semifreddo, sandwiches, milkshakes, sundaes, splits, and shaved ice. Gelato, granita, frozen yogurt, frozen custard, cremolada, cake, and velvet, too. There's ice milk, coolers, and floats, plus tacos, pies, pops, and paletas. There's even something called spoom, which might be our favorite of all—and there are probably others we forgot.

When you consider that frozen desserts can be made weeks in advance, be kept on hand for whenever, and can morph into a zillion other sweets, it's easy to run to your ice cream maker and jump in to the recipes. But it can also be a little daunting: Ice cream, like baking, is a science. To do it well, it helps to have a good recipe (or sixty) in your back pocket and to know what to do if things go awry.

The contributors whose recipes are featured here have made a lot of ice cream, and they don't run adorable ice cream shops either. They're home cooks who really like ice cream and who have learned how to make it well in their own kitchens. Their ice cream maker model might be the same as yours, and they know tempered eggs can get a little scrambled at times. They also have some pretty ingenious ideas in the flavor department.

Half of the recipes here are beloved by the Food52 community and have been made by many over and over. The other half are new, created by longtime Food52 contributor Cristina Sciarra. We knew she was a writer and cook with a day job in real estate development, but only after she signed on to dream up ice creams for this book did we learn that she also went to ice cream school—for *fun*! (I saw her study guide; there are a lot of numbers.) Her ice cream recipes are fail-proof, but—just as important—they taste good. Cristina knows that black pepper feta ice cream (page 139) isn't too wild for reality, and that beer ice cream (page 120) is the update that mud pies of yesteryear always needed.

But back to the scary part. With Cristina's help, and the smarts of our community, we've sprinkled tips throughout the book to help answer the questions you've always wondered about: What exactly is skim milk powder? My base curdled—what now?

There are also Genius tips, based on the Food52 series and (ahem, *New York Times* best-selling) book *Genius Recipes*, in which Food52 creative director Kristen Miglore unearths recipes from food luminaries that are so smart, they've changed the way we cook. These tips and ideas add to the collective brainpower found in these pages.

With its recipes and tips and practical science and ideas, we hope that this cookbook gives you really delicious ice cream. But also consider it permission to play. After all, an ice cream swirl is really just edible spin art. Once you know the ropes—and that you can make no-churn ice cream in any flavor (page 48)—why listen to us?

—Ali Slagle, books editor of Food52

Essential Reading & Riffing

Peppered throughout the book is a whole bunch of stuff besides ice cream recipes to help you make and eat and riff on the ice creams. For easy reference, here's a catalog of what's to come.

INGREDIENTS 101

MAKING & STORING

ADD-INS OR -ONS

Chocolate, Vanilla & Company

Naked Chocolate Ice Cream

Serves 2 chocolate lovers | From Barbara Reiss

3 cups (710ml)
half-and-half

1 cup (200g) sugar

¾ cup (65g)
unsweetened
cocoa powder

½ teaspoon
espresso powder

Pinch of kosher salt

3 tablespoons cornstarch

6 ounces (170g)
bittersweet chocolate,
chopped

3 tablespoons crème
de cacao or liqueur of
your choice

1 teaspoon vanilla extract

Imagine doing the breaststroke through a pool of glassy-smooth melted bittersweet chocolate. We can't give you that experience, but we *can* give you this unabashed and unadulterated chocolate ice cream.

Borrowing a smart technique from David Lebovitz's book *The Perfect Scoop*, Barbara uses cornstarch rather than eggs to thicken the pudding base so that the cocoa powder, chocolate, and vanilla extract come through in the end product "as if there were exclamation points around them."

For those who aren't chocolate-obsessed (are you really out there?), you can use this same technique—a cornstarch-thickened custard for an ice cream base—to make other flavors; Barbara has had great success with churning salted caramel custard, and we imagine a butterscotch or pumpkin pudding would be qualified candidates, too.

1. In a large saucepan, heat 2 cups (470ml) of the half-and-half, the sugar, cocoa powder, espresso powder, and salt over medium-low heat.

2. In a small bowl, whisk the cornstarch into the remaining 1 cup (240ml) of half-and-half until smooth, then stir into the cocoa mixture. Stir constantly over medium-high heat until the base thickens and begins to boil, about 5 minutes.

3. Off the heat, add the chocolate, crème de cacao, and vanilla, stirring until the chocolate melts and the mixture is very smooth. Cover the surface with wax paper and chill until cold, at least 2 hours but ideally overnight.

4. Scoop the ice cream base (it's thick) into an ice cream maker and churn it according to the manufacturer's instructions.

Mary's Healthy Ice Cream Sandwiches

This "recipe" comes from Amanda Hesser's father-in-law's girlfriend, Mary French: She uses a 3-inch (7.5cm) cookie cutter to make a circle in the middle of two slices of whole-wheat bread, toasts the circles, and, while the bread's still warm, smooshes a scoop of chocolate ice cream between the slices. Et voilà, an instant ice cream sandwich that's the ragtag cousin of pain au chocolat. Mary insists the wheat bread makes it healthy. We like Mary.

Homemade Sprinkles

Makes about 1½ cups (205g) | From Michelle Lopez

8 ounces (225g) confectioners' sugar, sifted

1 egg white, at room temperature

¾ teaspoon vanilla or any other extract, such as rose water or peppermint

¼ teaspoon kosher salt

Up to 3 food colorings of your choice

We'd have a hard time telling you what store-bought sprinkles are made of, let alone what they taste like. So for sprinkles that are flavorful and delicious enough to eat on their own, it's worth it (and pretty dang simple) to make them yourself. The best part? You can think about your ice cream's taste and appearance and choose your sprinkles' flavor and color scheme accordingly. Make it as elegant (dark sprinkles on chocolate ice cream) or as whimsical (a rainbow of sprinkles on mint-basil chip) as you'd like.

1. In the bowl of a stand mixer fitted with a paddle attachment (or using a handheld electric mixer), beat the confectioners' sugar, egg white, vanilla, and salt on low speed until combined.

2. Divide the paste among as many bowls as you have colors, tinting the paste in each bowl. Use a rubber spatula to stir the food coloring into the paste until it's an even hue. Adjust the amount of food coloring (if it's too thick) and sugar (if it's too thin) in small increments until you find a consistency that's squeezable.

3. Transfer the pastes to pastry bags fitted with small pastry tips such as Wilton's No. 2 or 3, or a zip-top plastic bag with one corner snipped. Pipe out long, thin lines on a baking sheet or jelly-roll pan. Repeat the process with the remaining colors and let the piped lines set, uncovered, in a dry place for 24 hours.

4. Once the piped lines have dried completely, use a bench scraper or a butter knife to chop them into short sprinkles.

5. Use immediately or store in an airtight container at room temperature for up to 1 month.

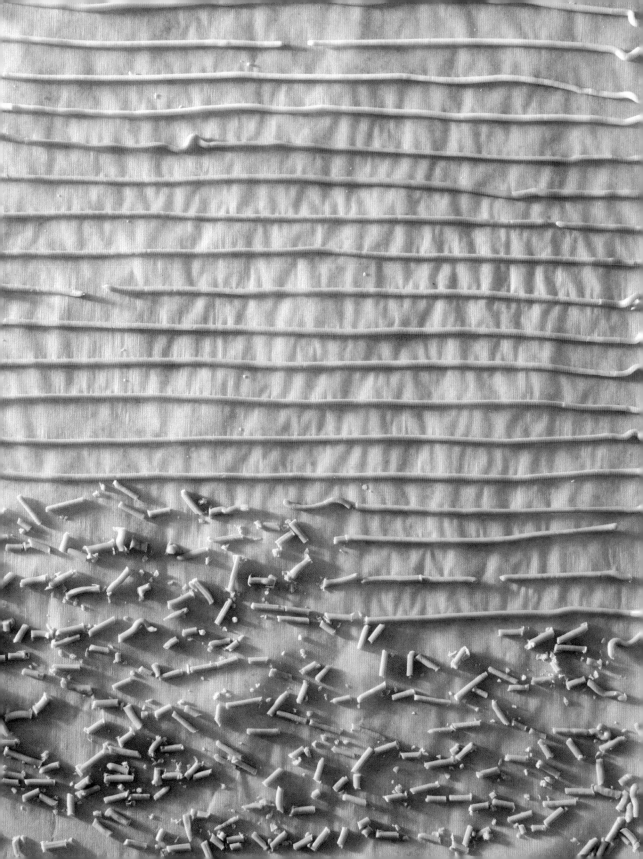

Two-Tone Fudge Pops

Makes 6 to 8 pops | From Merrill Stubbs

1 cup (240ml) heavy cream

1 cup (240ml) whole milk

3 ounces (85g) bittersweet chocolate, chopped

2 tablespoons light brown sugar

Large pinch of ground cinnamon

Large pinch of cayenne

3 ounces (85g) milk chocolate, chopped

Seeds from ½ vanilla bean

The best bite of these double-layer fudgesicles is right in the middle, so you get the spiced chocolate layer and the milky chocolate layer at the same time (it's sort of like getting the center of the Tootsie Pop without all the work). If you happen to have extras of either chocolate, Merrill says it's great in coffee, eaten by the spoonful, or in its own one-tone confection.

1. In a heavy saucepan, combine the heavy cream and milk over low heat.

2. In a heatproof bowl, combine the bittersweet chocolate, 1 tablespoon of the brown sugar, the cinnamon, and the cayenne.

3. In another heatproof bowl, combine the milk chocolate, remaining 1 tablespoon of brown sugar, and the vanilla seeds.

4. When the milk mixture is just about to boil, carefully pour half of it into each of the two bowls, whisking well to melt the chocolate and dissolve the sugar.

5. Pour the bittersweet chocolate mixture about halfway up the sides of each pop mold. Freeze until just beginning to set, 1 to 1½ hours. (In the meantime, cover and refrigerate the milk chocolate mixture.)

6. When the surface of the bittersweet chocolate mixture has firmed up, but the rest is still soft enough to insert a stick, give the milk chocolate mixture a quick whisk and divide it evenly among the molds (you know what to do with the leftovers!). Gently insert popsicle sticks, stabilizing them by pushing them a little bit into the bottom layer. Freeze the pops for several hours, until completely hard.

7. When ready to serve, dip the molds into a bowl of very hot water for a few seconds—the pops should slip out easily.

Better Chocolate Chunks

Makes enough for 3 to 4 cups (710 to 950ml) of ice cream
From Alice Medrich (adapted from *Seriously Bittersweet*)

4 ounces (115g) milk or dark chocolate, coarsely chopped

2 tablespoons water, plus extra as needed (optional, if you want fudgy chunks)

Recipes for homemade chocolate chip ice cream frequently recommend adding a chopped-up bar of chocolate—but frozen bits of even the highest-quality chocolate feel hard and gritty in your mouth. You can do better!

Ice cream manufacturers solve the problem by adding coconut oil to make the chocolate melt faster after you bite, but the oil dilutes the flavor. Here's a solution: If you want crunchy chunks or shards that shatter and then melt with a big burst of chocolate flavor (even in a rich chocolate ice cream), it's better to melt the chocolate, then chill it and chop it.

Melting the chocolate destroys the chocolate's temper, lowering its melting point and diminishing its ability to harden except when chilled. This just means that the chocolate will be brittle and crunchy in cold ice cream, but will soften in the warmth of your mouth, releasing its flavor more quickly than do frozen bits of a chocolate bar. Tricky but good, right?

You could even make fudgy instead of crunchy chunks by mixing the melted chocolate with water. Yes, you heard that right: It works so long as you add enough water for the cacao percentage of your chocolate. But more on that in the recipe.

Where to stick the chunks in the last few minutes of churning:

Naked Chocolate Ice Cream (page 2)

Philadelphia-Style Super Vanilla Ice Cream (page 16)

No-Churn Peanut Butter Curry Ice Cream (page 48)

Dark Chocolate–Rosemary Ice Cream (page 99)

Horchata Ice Cream (page 108)

Burnt Toast Ice Cream (page 148)

Beet Ice Milk (page 153)

Avocado Gelado (page 154)

1. In a stainless-steel bowl set over a saucepan of not quite simmering water, melt the chocolate and, if you want fudgy rather then crunchy chuncks, add the water, stirring frequently. (The higher the cacao percentage, the more water will be needed to prevent the chocolate mixture from seizing up. Start with 2 tablespoons of water for milk chocolate or dark chocolate with up to 60 percent cacao; for 66 to 72 percent cacao, at least an additional tablespoon of water will be needed.) Once the chocolate is melted, stir in a few teaspoons of warm water, as necessary, to make a smooth, fluid mixture; if it's stiff or curdled, add the water and stir until smooth.

2. Remove from the heat and pour the mixture onto a parchment- or foil-lined baking sheet. Spread into a thin, even layer.

3. Freeze the baking sheet until the chocolate is firm. Chop the chocolate into bits or shards, put them in a plastic bag, and return to the freezer until needed.

Olive Oil–Cacao Nib Gelato

Makes 1 quart (950ml) | From Amanda Hesser

¾ cup (150g) sugar

¾ cup (175ml) whole milk

Pinch of salt

4 egg yolks

6 tablespoons (90ml)
good-quality olive oil

2 tablespoons cacao nibs

If you have a bottle of olive oil you've been saving for a special occasion, bring it out now. Whisk the olive oil into a creamy gelato base and the floral, peppery flavors head just a smidge toward "sweet." Food52 contributor Yossy Arefi's turn on Amanda's recipe is to add cocoa nibs, crunchy like chocolate chips but fruity and bitter like olive oil. They're in no way necessary, but certainly a welcome bite in this smooth-as-aioli gelato.

1. In a saucepan, whisk together the sugar, milk, 6 tablespoons (90ml) water, and salt. Bring the mixture to a simmer over medium-low heat, stirring occasionally to dissolve the sugar. While the mixture is heating, in a large bowl, whisk together the egg yolks.

2. When the milk mixture has come to a gentle simmer, gradually whisk it into the egg yolks. Pour the mixture back into the saucepan and cook over medium-low heat, whisking constantly, until the mixture reaches 185°F (85°C) on a candy thermometer. Be careful not to let the mixture boil, which will scramble the eggs and ruin the base.

3. Remove from the heat, transfer to a bowl, and refrigerate to chill completely, at least 4 hours but ideally overnight. When the ice cream base is cold, whisk in the olive oil; the base will be thick and glossy.

4. Pour the chilled base into an ice cream maker and churn it according to the manufacturer's instructions. During the last minute of churning, add the cacao nibs.

Magic Shell

Former Food52 editor Marian Bull taught us how to make our own Magic Shell, that stuff you drizzled copiously over every scoop of ice cream as a kid, watched harden, then broke into like a little monster. For 1 cup (240ml) of the good stuff, chop 6 ounces (170g) good-quality chocolate (dark, preferably) and add it to a microwave-safe container with a scant ½ cup (110g) coconut oil. Melt in 30-second increments, stirring between each, until liquid. Pour over ice cream (or milkshakes). Then, magic! Magic Shell will stay liquid in a hot kitchen and solidify after sitting in a cold kitchen or the fridge. You can remelt it in the microwave.

Brooklyn Blackout Semifreddo Cake

Serves 6 to 8 | From Suzanne DeBrango

Cake

2 tablespoons unsalted butter

¼ cup (60ml) milk

2 cups (400g) sugar

8 eggs, at room temperature

¾ cup (95g) all-purpose flour

½ cup (40g) unsweetened cocoa powder (use black cocoa powder for an extra-blacked-out cake)

1 teaspoon baking powder

1 teaspoon kosher salt

1 teaspoon vanilla extract

Semifreddo

7 ounces (200g) dark chocolate (70% cacao), chopped

2 teaspoons espresso powder

½ cup (100g) sugar

2 eggs

2 teaspoons vanilla extract

1⅓ cups (315ml) heavy cream

2 tablespoons cream cheese, at room temperature

The original Brooklyn Blackout Cake was created by Ebinger's Bakery in Brooklyn during World War II—it got its name from all the blackout drills in the area at the time. Rumor has it that right before the bakery went out of business in the 1970s, diehards stocked up and put lots of these fudgy pudding layer cakes in their freezers for safekeeping. This rendition isn't just an ice cream version of the classic, though. Nor is it your run-of-the-mill ice cream or chocolate cake. When a rich semifreddo custard (instead of pudding) is schmeared between layers of sponge cake, you get ice cream–like stripes of filling straight from the freezer, which become even fudgier after the cake thaws a tad.

1. To make the cake, heat the oven to 350°F (175°C). Grease a baking sheet, line it with parchment, butter the parchment, and sprinkle with sugar. Melt the butter with the milk in the microwave, about 45 seconds. Beat the sugar and eggs on medium-high speed until the mixture is pale yellow, tripled in volume, and thick, about 8 minutes. With the mixer running, slowly add the milk and butter.

2. Sift together the flour, cocoa powder, baking powder, and salt, then fold it into the egg mixture; there should be no lumps. Fold in the vanilla.

3. Pour the batter into the prepared baking sheet and spread it evenly. Bake until a toothpick inserted comes out clean, 20 to 25 minutes. Cool for a couple of minutes, then run a knife around the edges to loosen it. Invert the pan onto a wire rack, remove the parchment, and let cool completely.

4. To make the semifreddo, in a metal or glass bowl set over a pot of slowly simmering water, melt the chocolate and espresso powder, then remove from the heat. Keep the pot simmering—you'll need it again!

5. In a metal or glass bowl, whisk together the sugar, eggs, and vanilla. Place the bowl over the simmering water and whisk until it thickens and the sugar dissolves. Off the water, continue whisking until the mixture doubles in volume and the whisk leaves a ribbon when lifted from the bowl. Whisk in the melted chocolate and let cool for about 10 minutes.

6. Whisk together the heavy cream and cream cheese until whipped. Fold the whipped cream into the chocolate mixture in 2 additions, just until incorporated.

CONTINUED

Ganache

6 tablespoons (90ml) heavy cream

4 ounces (115g) dark chocolate (70% cacao), broken into small pieces

1 tablespoon light corn syrup (optional)

7. Line a 10-inch (25cm) loaf pan with plastic wrap, leaving extra plastic hanging over the long sides of the pan.

8. Cut the cake into 3 pieces that will fit into the loaf pan (you will use the extra cake for the crumb topping). Place the first piece of cake into the pan. Top with half of the semifreddo, followed by the second piece of cake, the remaining semifreddo, and finally, the third piece of cake. Fold the hanging plastic over the top, and freeze overnight or for up to a week. Wrap the remaining cake in plastic wrap; you will need it for serving.

9. On the day you want to serve the cake, make the ganache: Heat the heavy cream in a pot over medium heat until scalding. Add the chocolate and corn syrup. Remove from the heat, let the mixture sit for approximately 5 minutes, and then stir until smooth. Let cool to room temperature.

10. Crumble the remaining cake with your hands or a food processor.

11. Use the plastic overhang to transfer the cake to a serving plate. Remove the plastic from the cake.

12. Spread a thin layer of ganache on the sides of the cake, press the cake crumbs on the sides, spread another thin layer of ganache on top, and freeze until firm, 2 to 4 hours (or up to 2 weeks, well wrapped). Let sit at room temperature for about 10 minutes before serving.

Philadelphia-Style Super Vanilla Ice Cream

Makes 1 quart (950ml) | From Cristina Sciarra

1 ¾ cups (415ml)
heavy cream

1 ¼ cups (300ml)
whole milk

½ cup plus 2 tablespoons
(125g) sugar

3 tablespoons skim
milk powder

1 tablespoon dark rum

1 vanilla bean, split
lengthwise

1 teaspoon vanilla extract

Because Philadelphia-style ice cream avoids eggs—and therefore cooking a custard—it has more lift than traditional ice cream. So this vanilla rendition is like a vanilla Frosty meets whipped cream: The flavor is full-on vanilla and dairy (with a wink of rum), so be sure to use the best ingredients you come across. You'll want to eat this one right from the canister (by which we mean dollop it on pie) or within a few days of churning. Otherwise, the ice cream will go crunchy.

1. In a pot, whisk together the heavy cream, milk, sugar, milk powder, and rum. Add the vanilla bean seeds and pod and vanilla extract. Bring the mixture to a simmer over medium-low heat before whisking to dissolve the sugar.

2. Remove from the heat, let cool, then chill the base completely in the refrigerator for at least 4 hours but ideally overnight. Pass the chilled base through a fine-mesh sieve set over a bowl and discard the vanilla bean pod.

3. Pour the chilled base into an ice cream maker and churn it according to the manufacturer's instructions.

4. Serve the ice cream straight from the machine. You could spoon into a container and freeze overnight, but the consistency won't be quite as light. If frozen, let sit for about 10 minutes to soften before scooping.

Know Your Dash from Your Splash

As in this vanilla ice cream, a bit of booze is added to a base not (just) for flavor but to help with consistency. Alcohol lowers the freezing point of ice cream, so it'll have a harder time toughening up in the freezer. But don't go glugging bottles of wine or rum into every ice cream base: 1 tablespoon per 1-quart (950ml) batch is the safe zone. Any more than 2 or 3 tablespoons and that ice cream will be a sloppy mess, never to take shape and graduate to sophomore year.

Fresh Ricotta Ice Cream

Makes a scant 1 quart (950ml) | From Pat Aresty

1²/₃ cups (410g) fresh whole milk ricotta

3 ounces (85g) cream cheese

1 cup (240ml) whole milk

1 cup (200g) sugar

2 tablespoons dark rum

1 teaspoon grated lemon zest

½ teaspoon vanilla extract

⅛ teaspoon kosher salt

1 cup (240ml) heavy cream

2 to 3 tablespoons chopped candied citrus peel (such as orange, lemon, or citron)

2 to 3 tablespoons chopped pistachios

2 to 3 tablespoons chopped bittersweet chocolate

When Pat Aresty tasted ricotta gelato for the first time in Florence, she experienced "gelato nirvana," then promptly took it upon herself to re-create the dessert. She used a ricotta ice cream in *Gourmet* magazine as her launchpad, throwing in candied citrus peel, chopped pistachios, and chocolate to mimic the filling of another classic Italian dessert: cannoli. With a homemade sugar cone wafer (page 20) to stand in for the cannoli shell, you might as well be in a piazza in Palermo.

Both homemade and purchased whole milk ricotta are fine—as is sheep's milk. But if your ricotta is grainy, your final ice cream will be, too.

1. Blend both cheeses, the milk, sugar, rum, lemon zest, vanilla, and salt until smooth. Add the heavy cream and blend until the base is just combined.

2. Pour the base into an ice cream maker and churn it according to the manufacturer's instructions. During the last minute of churning, add the candied citrus peel, pistachios, and chocolate.

Balsamic Butterscotch Sauce

If you like salted caramel (page 30), then you'll be praising this sauce of Liz Larkin's at first spoonful. It takes a savory surprise to butterscotch, which is caramel but with brown sugar in the mix. For 2 cups (475ml) of sauce, in a small saucepan, combine ⅓ cup (75g) salted butter, 1 cup (220g) packed light brown sugar, ⅓ cup (65g) granulated sugar, and ⅔ cup (160ml) heavy cream and cook over low heat, stirring, until the sugar dissolves. Boil the sauce over medium heat, whisking continuously for 5 minutes. Off the heat, stir in 2 tablespoons white balsamic vinegar. Taste and add up to a tablespoon more. The sauce will thicken as it cools and keep in the fridge for up to 2 weeks. Pour it on ice cream (nuke it so that it's pourable, though it doesn't taste bad cold!) but also bananas, cake, ricotta, a spoon.

Sugar Cones & Other Shapes

Makes 10 to 12 cones | From Cristina Sciarra

6 tablespoons (75g) granulated sugar

2 tablespoons light brown sugar

2 egg whites

3 tablespoons whole milk

3 tablespoons unsalted butter, melted but not hot

½ teaspoon vanilla extract

⅛ teaspoon kosher salt

½ cup (60g) flour

Whereas boxed sugar cones could be confused with thin cardboard, these are sweet, buttery, and slightly caramelized. And you get to decorate them any which way: Dip edges in Magic Shell (page 10) and then sprinkle on sprinkles (page 4), caramelized ginger, or chopped nuts. Or puddle the Magic Shell or caramel (page 85) or butterscotch (page 19) on the inside. You can even add some flare to the batter by adding ground ginger, cocoa powder, orange zest, or poppy seeds.

Folding these dainty cones does take some practice to master: After baking thin, tuile-style cookies, you fold them up while they're still hot from the oven and then let them crisp up. They taste so good that even if the shapes are a little wonky, you can stick a couple into your bowl and call them abstract art.

1. Heat the oven to 350°F (175°C). Line a baking sheet with parchment or a silicone baking mat, and lightly spray with oil.

2. In a large bowl, whisk together both sugars and the egg whites. Whisk in the milk, butter, vanilla, and salt, followed by the flour, until smooth. (The batter can be refrigerated in an airtight container for up to 3 days. Bring to room temperature before using.)

3. Now, decide what shape you're after: For cups or cannoli-esque tubes, spoon the batter onto the prepared baking sheet, then use a small offset spatula to form thin, even discs 6 inches (15cm) in diameter. For more traditional pyramid cones, spoon the batter into half-moon shapes. Bake for 8 to 10 minutes, or until golden.

4. Remove from the oven and, working quickly, use an offset spatula to carefully lift the shapes off the baking sheet, then use your hands and tongs (wear plastic gloves if the shapes are too hot) to immediately form them (bribe a friend or two to help you). To make cups, fit the discs into lightly sprayed muffin tins; for cannoli-esque tubes, roll up the circles like loose cigars; and for cones, take a half-moon and grab each end of the straight edge. Pull the ends toward the center, tightening and overlapping, so that the curved part of the half-moon is now the top of the cone. (If the discs become too hard to mold, move the baking sheet back to the oven for 30 seconds to a minute.) Use a cool baking sheet for the next batch.

5. Cool completely before decorating. While best fresh, the cones can be stored at room temperature in an airtight container for up to 2 days.

Malted Vanilla Ice Cream with Chocolate-Covered Pretzels

Makes a generous quart (950ml) | From Emily Vikre

Chocolate-Covered Pretzel Bits

8 ounces (225g) dark chocolate, finely chopped

1 tablespoon unsalted butter, at room temperature

¾ cup (40g) salted pretzel sticks

Malted Vanilla Ice Cream

1¾ cups (415ml) heavy cream

1¼ cups (300ml) whole milk

½ cup (100g) sugar

⅓ cup (80ml) light corn syrup

¼ teaspoon kosher salt

6 egg yolks, lightly beaten

⅔ cup (95g) malted milk powder

1 teaspoon vanilla extract

Think of an old-fashioned pharmacy—the kind with the soda jerks, malts, and long pretzel rods in tall glass containers. Now wrap all those feelings in vanilla ice cream, and you get this: a malted milk ice cream with salty, chocolate-covered pretzel pieces shooting through it. Bonus: The chocolate keeps the pretzels from getting soggy.

1. To make the pretzel bits, line a rimmed baking sheet with wax paper. Melt the chocolate in the microwave in 30-second increments, stirring between each. Stir in the butter until the mixture is smooth.

2. Break up the pretzels into little pieces. Drop the pretzel bits into the chocolate and stir until evenly coated. Using a fork, lift the pretzel bits out of the chocolate and separate them on the prepared baking sheet. Refrigerate until hard, 20 to 30 minutes. Store in an airtight container at room temperature for up to a week.

3. To make the ice cream, in a heavy saucepan, whisk together the heavy cream, milk, ¼ cup (50g) of the sugar, the corn syrup, and salt. Simmer over medium-low heat, then turn the heat to low. Meanwhile, in a medium bowl, whisk together the egg yolks, malt powder, and remaining ¼ cup (50g) sugar.

4. Whisk a ladleful of the hot cream into the egg yolks (vigorously!) to temper them. Repeat with one or two more ladlefuls. Pour the egg mixture into the pan with the rest of the cream mixture.

5. Stir the mixture constantly over medium-low heat until it has thickened to a custard texture and coats the back of a spoon. Pass the custard through a fine-mesh sieve into a large metal bowl, then stir in the vanilla. Refrigerate to chill completely, at least 4 hours but ideally overnight.

6. Pour the chilled base into an ice cream maker and churn it according to the manufacturer's instructions. During the last minute of churning, add the pretzel bits.

S'mores Ice Cream

Makes about 1 quart (950ml) | From Phyllis Grant

S'mores Chunks

12 graham crackers (honey or plain, but not cinnamon)

2 cups (100g) mini marshmallows

10 ounces (285g) bittersweet chocolate, broken apart or chopped

Marshmallow Ice Cream

1½ cups (355ml) half-and-half

4 egg yolks

¼ teaspoon kosher salt

2 cups (100g) mini marshmallows

1½ cups (355ml) heavy cream

When Phyllis was developing this recipe, she toyed with the idea of brown butter–graham cracker crumbs to take it upscale, but her tasters said no—s'mores ice cream is meant to be sweet and full of hefty chunks and creamy swirls. The final recipe isn't shy about how sweet it is, nor is it embarrassed about the messiness involved. There's a wonderfully sticky web of marshmallow and lots of bittersweet chocolate rippled over graham crackers, which then get smooshed into a toasty marshmallow ice cream. It's the sort of thing you might dribble down your bathing suit—and we encourage you to do so.

1. To make the chunks, heat the broiler. Line a baking sheet with parchment paper. Arrange 6 of the graham crackers on the baking sheet so that they're touching completely. Cover evenly with the marshmallows. Broil. Don't walk away. Rotate the baking sheet for even broiling. Remove when the marshmallows are just starting to burn.

2. Immediately sandwich the marshmallows with the remaining 6 graham crackers.

3. Melt the chocolate in the microwave in 30-second increments, stirring frequently.

4. Pour the melted chocolate over the graham cracker sandwiches. Spread the chocolate all over and let it drip over the edges. Freeze until firm.

5. Chop the chocolate-covered sandwiches into bite-size pieces. They will fall apart and crumble. This leads to all kinds of wonderful textures and flavors in the ice cream. Place in a jar or a freezer-safe plastic bag in the freezer.

6. To make the ice cream, set up an ice bath by placing several handfuls of ice in a large bowl (you'll add the water later). Place a smaller bowl inside the larger bowl. Rest a fine-mesh sieve on top.

7. In a bowl, whisk together the half-and-half, egg yolks, and salt.

8. Heat the broiler. Spread the marshmallows evenly on the bottom of an ovenproof pot. Broil until the tops of the marshmallows are nicely browned and just about to burn, about 2 minutes.

CONTINUED

9. Transfer the pot to the stove top and pour the heavy cream over the marshmallows. Whisk constantly over medium heat, until the marshmallow cream is just about to boil. Slowly whisk the hot marshmallow cream into the egg yolk mixture, then pour back into the pot and continue cooking, stirring the whole time with a wooden spoon. The base is done when you drag your finger across the back of a coated spoon and a trail lingers.

10. Pass the base through the prepared sieve and into the smaller bowl. Fill the larger bowl with water until it rises to the level of the base. Once cool, cover and refrigerate overnight.

11. Pour the chilled base into an ice cream maker and churn it according to the manufacturer's instructions. Spoon the ice cream into a container, fold in at least 2 cups (190g) of the s'mores chunks, and freeze for a few hours, or overnight. Eat!

Store-Bought Shortcut

The s'mores chunks are good enough to be sold in a candy shop. Keep them in the freezer, soften some store-bought vanilla ice cream, then mix in some of those chunks from the freezer. You'll have yourself a very fine semi-homemade ice cream.

Chocolate Tacos

Makes 6 to 8 | From Molly Yeh

Taco Shells

⅔ cup (85g) all-purpose flour

½ cup (100g) sugar

⅛ teaspoon kosher salt

2 tablespoons unsalted butter, melted, plus more for the skillet

¼ cup (60ml) milk

¼ teaspoon almond extract

½ teaspoon vanilla extract

2 egg whites

Fillings and Toppings

10 ounces (285g) dark chocolate chips

3 tablespoons coconut oil

4 to 6 cups (950ml to 1.4L) ice cream, softened (store-bought Choco Tacos have fudge-swirled vanilla ice cream)

½ cup (60g) crushed nuts, plus any other desired toppings

With these chocolate tacos, it's your taco party so you can do what you want. You can spoon whatever ice cream flavor you desire into soft, chewy shells (that you shape by hanging over books, but not this one!), then top with Picasso-like splatters of chocolate and crushed nuts—or sprinkles (page 4) or brittle (page 50) or gummy bears. You get the idea.

The shells are a love child of eggy crêpes and soft flour tortillas—and the secret star of this taco. You can make the shells a day in advance and have guests fill their own, or you can make the tacos entirely in advance and keep them in the freezer.

1. To make the taco shells, cover 6 to 8 hardcover books that are 1 inch (2.5cm) thick with parchment paper. Stand them up vertically, spine up. These are your shell molds.

2. In a bowl, whisk together the flour, sugar, and salt. In a separate bowl, whisk together the butter, milk, 1 tablespoon water, almond extract, and vanilla, followed by the egg whites. Whisk the wet ingredients into the dry ingredients.

3. Warm a nonstick skillet over medium heat. Butter the skillet and then spoon in 2½ tablespoons of batter. Spread the batter gently with the back of a spoon or offset spatula so you have an even circle. Cook until slightly brown on the bottom, 3 to 5 minutes. Flip and cook until slightly brown on the second side, 1 to 2 minutes more. With a spatula, gently fold the shell over the spine of the book and let cool. Repeat with the remaining batter, adding butter to the pan as needed.

4. Melt the chocolate chips and coconut oil in the microwave in 30-second increments, stirring between each. Let cool slightly.

5. Fill the taco shells with ice cream, drizzle with as much chocolate as you wish, top with the nuts, and enjoy! You can freeze uncovered for a few minutes to let the chocolate harden; the tacos will also keep, wrapped in plastic wrap, in the freezer for up to 2 months.

Salted Caramel Ice Cream Milkshakes

Makes about 1 quart (950ml) ice cream and, in turn, many child-size milkshakes | From Amanda Hesser

1¼ cups (250g) sugar

2 teaspoons light corn syrup

2 cups (475ml) heavy cream

2 cups (475ml) whole milk, plus more for blending the milkshakes

10 egg yolks

½ teaspoon fleur de sel

This recipe transforms salted caramel ice cream into a nostalgic shake that should be neither milky nor solid, but "ploppy," as Amanda explained to her kids the first time she made it with a kid-friendly blender "Santa" gave them. While you could make this shake with any very good store-bought salted caramel ice cream, you'll notice the difference when you make this one, an adaption from one at New York's Eleven Madison Park. It has an intensely dark, rich caramelly flavor you can get only from leaving the caramel on the stove just a moment longer than you'd deem a good idea. If you're not making milkshakes, sprinkle the ice cream with fleur de sel just before serving.

1. In a heavy saucepan, combine ¾ cup (150g) of the sugar and the corn syrup. Do not stir. Cook over medium-high heat until it's a dark caramel, about 5 minutes, swirling to distribute the sugar as it begins to brown. Add the heavy cream, stirring to get all the bits stuck on the bottom of the pan, then slowly add the milk and continue to stir. The caramel will harden. Bring to a boil, then simmer, stirring, just until the caramel has dissolved.

2. In a large bowl, whisk together the remaining ½ cup (100g) sugar, the egg yolks, and fleur de sel. Whisk a little caramel cream into the egg mixture to temper, then pour the egg mixture into the remaining caramel cream and mix. Pass the mixture through a fine-mesh sieve into a bowl. Let cool completely in the refrigerator, preferably overnight.

3. Pour the chilled base into an ice cream maker and churn it according to the manufacturer's instructions.

4. When you're ready to make the milkshakes, just drop a large scoop of ice cream per person in the blender. Add enough milk to almost cover the scoops—usually ½ to 1 cup (120 to 240ml) does the trick. Turn on the blender—bbrrrrrrrrr! Done!

Sorry, Kids

For a boozier rendition, decrease the milk to ¼ to ½ cup (60 to 120ml) and splash in ¼ cup (60ml)—or more—of whiskey or rum before blending.

How to Make a Milkshake Every Which Way

Whoever you are, you can't possibly mess up a milkshake, and that's a fact. If you mess up the ratio of milk to ice cream, just add more of either one until you have the right consistency. The worst thing that can happen is that you end up with a larger milkshake than you were expecting, and that's a pretty great "worst thing."

Here's how to make the milkshake you always wanted, with whatever you have on hand.

1. Get out your blender and ponder a deep question: Do you prefer icy shakes or silky shakes? If you prefer icy shakes, you'll want to crush a handful of ice cubes in the blender or by hand before you start. If you want a smoother shake, let the ice cream sit out on the counter for a few minutes.

2. Plop in several scoops of ice cream (we recommend one or two per person). Choose any flavor you want, but make sure it's high quality, as the ice cream will determine not only the flavor, but also the texture of your shake. For our purposes, sorbet and frozen yogurt also fall under the broad umbrella of ice cream.

3. Next comes the milk. You can use whole, skim, or even dairy-free. The richer the milk, the richer the shake. Pour in a bit of milk, then blend and test the viscosity. If your shake is too thick, add more milk; if it's too thin, add more ice cream. Rocket science, this is not.

4. Finally, the add-ins! This is an opportunity to transform whatever flavor of ice cream you already have into something new and exciting—see some ideas at left. Throw them in all at once or go for more textural variety and add the crunchy toppings when you're almost finished blending.

5. Blend it all together. It will only take a few seconds in a powerful blender.

6. Top with whipped cream and other garnishes of your choice. Sip through a large straw, or use a spoon to dig into a thicker shake.

Add-in ideas:

Chocolate syrup, strawberry syrup, or vanilla extract

Maple syrup, ground espresso beans, malted milk powder

A spoonful or two of sweetened condensed milk, almond butter, tahini, or chocolate-hazelnut spread

Frozen fruit

Cookies like graham crackers or Oreos

Any candy bar, broken into pieces

Booze

Saltine Cracker–Brownie Ice Cream Sandwich

Makes about 16 ice cream sandwiches | From Mandy Lee

Crackers

50 to 60 salted saltines or soda crackers

2 tablespoons unsalted butter, melted

Brownie

½ cup (85g) semisweet chocolate chips

½ cup (110g) unsalted butter, cut into cubes

½ cup (100g) granulated sugar

½ cup (110g) packed brown sugar

2 eggs

1½ tablespoons ground espresso beans

1 teaspoon vanilla extract

⅔ cup (85g) all-purpose flour

2 tablespoons unsweetened cocoa powder

½ teaspoon sea salt

No-Churn Ice Cream

¾ cup plus 1 tablespoon (240g) sweetened condensed milk

1½ teaspoons vanilla extract

1½ tablespoons dark rum

1⅓ cups (315ml) heavy cream

It's hard to have qualms about ice cream sandwiches, but we've got two: They can be overly sweet and very large. But in swapping unwieldy cookies for saltine crackers, both problems go poof. The salt from the crackers balances out the almost-marshmallowy no-churn ice cream (adapted from a recipe in Martha Stewart's *Everyday Food*) and the densely fudgy brownie layer. That's right—what ice cream sandwich have you had with a brownie layer?

1. Layer the bottom of a 9-inch (23cm) square baking pan with crackers. Count how many you have and multiply that number by 2. Once you've figured out how many crackers you'll need, brush the crackers on both sides with the butter.

2. To make the brownie, heat the oven to 350°F (175°C). Adjust the oven racks to the middle and lower positions. Oil the baking pan and line it with parchment paper, leaving extra parchment hanging. Have a baking sheet ready, too.

3. In a big bowl, melt the chocolate chips and butter in the microwave in 30-second increments, stirring between each. Whisk in both sugars, the eggs, ground espresso, and vanilla until smooth and slightly fluffy. Sift in the flour, cocoa powder, and salt. Fold the ingredients together with a spatula or whisk until smooth.

4. Pour the brownie batter into the prepared pan and smooth the top. Arrange half of the crackers on top of the batter. If a whole cracker doesn't fit at the edge, just cut the cracker with a sharp knife into the exact size. Once you have completely covered the brownie batter with crackers, scatter the rest of the crackers on the baking sheet.

5. Place the brownie-cracker on the oven's middle rack and the crackers on the lower rack. Bake until the brownie-cracker is slightly underdone, about 25 minutes; a wooden skewer inserted into the center should come out moist with wet crumbs. Take out the crackers as well.

CONTINUED

6. Let the brownie-cracker cool for 10 minutes, then transfer the pan to the freezer for 30 minutes. The brownie-cracker should be completely cold before you continue. (They will keep, tightly wrapped in plastic, in the freezer for up to 1 week.)

7. Transfer the brownie-cracker to a work surface. Line the pan with another piece of parchment, invert the brownie-cracker, and remove the first layer of parchment. Place back in the pan, cracker layer facing down. Take note of where the uneven crackers are so that you can match the top layer of crackers to the bottom layer and make even cuts later. Return to the freezer while you make the ice cream.

8. To make the ice cream, in a small bowl, combine the condensed milk, vanilla, and rum.

9. In the bowl of a stand mixer fitted with a whisk attachment (or a handheld electric mixer), whisk the heavy cream on medium-high speed until soft peaks form, about 3 minutes. Gently fold the condensed milk mixture into the whipped cream just until combined.

10. Pour the ice cream on top of the brownie-cracker and smooth the top with a spoon. Arrange the remaining crackers on top, making sure to arrange them so that they match the bottom layer of crackers for easy cutting. Return the pan to the freezer to harden for at least 8 hours, or up to overnight.

11. Cut between the crackers to form little sandwiches. Wrap each mini sandwich with plastic wrap and freeze for up to 2 weeks.

Nutty

Brown Butter Pecan Ice Cream

Makes about 1 quart (950ml) | From Mrs. Mehitabel

1 cup (225g) salted butter

1 tablespoon plus 1 teaspoon tapioca starch or cornstarch

2 cups (475ml) whole milk

1/2 cup (120ml) heavy cream

2/3 cup (150g) packed brown sugar

2 tablespoons tapioca syrup or light corn syrup

2 tablespoons sour cream

1/2 cup to 1 cup (50 to 100g) roasted pecan pieces

The first time Mrs. Mehitabel made this no-custard ice cream, she and her husband scooped it into cones, took it on a late afternoon walk, and entirely forgot about the plans they had with friends. So consider this your warning: The distinctly nutty brown butter base, the brown sugar cut with just a dab of sour cream, and the crunchy pecans will make you forget all your responsibilities.

1. Brown the butter: In a large saucepan over medium heat, bring the butter to a boil, then let simmer until it's dark brown (try not to burn it!). Off the heat, let sit until the brown solids settle at the bottom; then, pour out the clarified butter, leaving just the solids in the pan. Reserve the clarified butter for another use.

2. Whisk together the tapioca starch and 2 tablespoons of the milk to form a slurry.

3. Add the remaining milk, the heavy cream, brown sugar, and tapioca syrup to the butter solids. Bring to a boil over medium-low heat, then stir constantly for 4 minutes. Whisk in the slurry, turn the heat to low, and continue cooking for just a minute, until the mixture no longer tastes of raw starch. Off the heat, whisk in the sour cream.

4. Let the ice cream base cool, then chill completely in the refrigerator for at least 4 hours but ideally overnight. Your base may look slightly grainy—don't worry.

5. Pour the chilled base into an ice cream maker and churn it according to the manufacturer's instructions.

6. Spoon the ice cream into a container, stir in the pecans, and freeze.

Peanut Butter Ice Cream with Concord Grape Sauce

Makes 1½ quarts (1.4L) | From Lisa Canducci Bailey

Grape Sauce

2 pounds (900g) Concord grapes, stemmed

2 tablespoons turbinado sugar

Juice of 1 lemon

Pinch of sea salt

Peanut Butter Ice Cream

1 cup (250g) natural peanut butter, stirred in the jar

1 cup (240ml) whole milk

½ cup (100g) turbinado sugar

1 tablespoon honey

½ vanilla bean

2 cups (475ml) heavy cream

Don't let Concords' short season stop you from eating this spin on a PB&J beyond the start of the school year. The recipe's creator has incorporated mashed bananas into the peanut butter base, and suggests folding in chopped dark chocolate if that's your thing. She's even ditched the sauce and swirled jam right into the ice cream. We're dreaming of a hot honey (see below) swirl. It's all good. Just like a PB&J.

1. To make the sauce, in a saucepan over medium heat, gently simmer the grapes, ¼ cup (60ml) water, sugar, lemon juice, and salt, partially covered, until the grapes have burst, 15 minutes.

2. Uncover the pan, turn the heat to low, and continue to simmer until the mixture has thickened enough to coat the back of a spoon, about 10 minutes more.

3. Pass the sauce through a fine-mesh sieve into a bowl, discarding the skins and seeds, and refrigerate until chilled, about 20 minutes.

4. To make the ice cream, in a large bowl, whisk together the peanut butter, milk, sugar, and honey until smooth. Add the seeds of the vanilla bean and heavy cream, and whisk until combined. Chill the base completely in the refrigerator for at least 1 hour but ideally overnight.

5. Pour the chilled base into an ice cream maker and churn it according to the manufacturer's instructions.

6. Serve the ice cream straight from the machine, like soft serve. Spoon sauce over the scoops. If you choose to freeze the ice cream before serving, know that it won't be quite as creamy.

Make Your Honey Hot

You'll always find a bottle of Mike's Hot Honey in the Food52 pantry, but making your own spicy-sweet honey (or hot rosemary honey, or hot lemon honey) is simple: Grab a glass jar with a tight-fitting lid and add 2 to 4 halved hot chiles and whatever other flavors you like. How much you add depends on the intensity of your ingredients and what else is going into the honey. Pour in ½ cup (170g) mild honey, stir, then add another ½ cup (170g) honey. Seal the jar and let it sit for 1 to 2 weeks—the longer, the stronger. Strain the honey and store it in a glass jar. Drizzle over ice cream, oatmeal, fried chicken, pizza, pie—give it to loved ones, hoard it.

Hot Honey–Candied Black Walnut Ice Cream

Makes 1 quart (950ml) | From Cristina Sciarra

1 cup (100g) black walnuts

2 tablespoons hot honey

2 tablespoons unsalted butter, melted

2 cups (475ml) heavy cream

1 cup (240ml) whole milk

½ cup (35g) skim milk powder

¾ cup (150g) sugar

4 egg yolks

If butter pecan is eternal spring, this is summer rain: shameless and toasty. Black walnuts (earthier than their more faint, familiar friends) are baked in melted butter and hot honey (to make your own, see page 41). Half of the caramelly, spicy walnuts are blended into a cream base for dark peppery bitterness throughout, and the rest get swirled in before freezing. If you can't find black walnuts, regular ones or even pecans can work—just don't expect quite the same storm of flavors.

1. Heat the oven to 350°F (175°C). Scatter the walnuts across a baking sheet. Pour the hot honey and melted butter over and toss until evenly coated. Bake until fragrant and toasted, about 8 minutes—watch them carefully so they don't burn. Cool, coarsely chop, and set aside.

2. In a pot, whisk together the heavy cream, milk, milk powder, and ½ cup (100g) of the sugar. Bring to a simmer over medium-low heat, then remove from the heat.

3. In a bowl, whisk together the egg yolks with the remaining ¼ cup (50g) sugar for 1 minute. Gradually whisk the milk mixture into the yolks.

4. Pour the mixture back into the pot and cook over medium-low heat, stirring occasionally, until it thickens enough to coat the back of a spoon.

5. Add half of the chopped walnuts to the base. Blend until smooth, about 1 minute. Let the warm base steep for 30 minutes, then pass it through a fine-mesh sieve into a bowl. Chill completely in the refrigerator for at least 5 hours but ideally overnight.

6. Pour the chilled base into an ice cream maker and churn it according to the manufacturer's instructions. During the last minute of churning, add the remaining chopped walnuts.

Halvah Paletas

Makes 10 pops | From Cristina Sciarra

12 ounces (340g) halvah

2 cups (475ml) unsweetened almond milk

½ cup (170g) honey

¼ cup (60g) tahini, stirred in the jar

1 teaspoon vanilla extract

1 teaspoon almond extract

1 teaspoon ground cinnamon

If you're looking for a fudgy pop, keep walking—to page 7, perhaps. With a base made from almond milk and cinnamon, the first bite will remind you of an icy horchata, but the buttery halvah crystals give a richness rare in an ice pop. It's the sort of thing we'd be happy to eat off a stick (maybe drizzled with Magic Shell, page 10, and sesame seeds) and just as happy to slurp melted through a straw.

1. In a high-powered blender, combine 4 ounces (115g) of the halvah, the almond milk, honey, tahini, vanilla, almond extract, and cinnamon and blend until smooth, about 2 minutes.

2. Chop the remaining 8 ounces (225g) halvah and divide among pop molds. Pour the almond milk mixture evenly among the molds.

3. Freeze for at least 5 hours before serving.

Genius Tip: Brain Unfreezing

Ice Creams, Sorbets & Gelati: The Definitive Guide, no surprise, has a lot of ice cream recipes. It also has four quick cures for the common brain freeze: (1) Drink a glass of water to thaw out the chilly areas. (2) Press your tongue against the roof of your mouth to warm up blood vessels. (3) Trap your nose and mouth with your hand and breathe quickly to warm your face. (4) Eat slower, in smaller bites. (Ha!)

Marzipan Semifreddo with Citrus

Serves 6 to 8 | From Cristina Sciarra

1 cup (240ml) heavy
cream, well chilled

4 eggs, separated,
at room temperature

2/3 cup (135g) sugar

1/4 teaspoon cream
of tartar

1/8 teaspoon kosher salt

1/2 cup (155g) marzipan

1/4 cup (60ml) freshly
squeezed lemon juice

2 teaspoons almond
extract

1 teaspoon grated
lemon zest

1 teaspoon grated
orange zest

Here, almond is as fluffy as you typically know it to be crunchy. That's because marzipan is smoothed into a light-as-air egg yolk custard (as the Italians say, *zabaglione*), which is then gingerly mixed with meringue, followed by whipped cream. After freezing—that's right, no ice cream maker needed—it's only firm enough to just hold together. The citrus is there to counter some of the plushness, but not too much.

1. In a large bowl, beat the heavy cream on medium-high speed until soft peaks form, 3 to 4 minutes. Refrigerate.

2. Bring a medium pot with 1½ inches (4cm) of water to a simmer. Combine the egg whites, ⅓ cup (65g) of the sugar, the cream of tartar, and salt in a large heatproof bowl and set it on top of the simmering water. Using the electric mixer, beat the mixture on medium-high speed until opaque and foamy, 3 to 4 minutes. Off the water, continue mixing until the meringue is stiff and glossy, about 8 minutes more. Set the meringue aside. Keep the pot of water simmering—you'll need it again!

3. In a separate large heatproof bowl, combine the marzipan, lemon juice, almond extract, and remaining ⅓ cup (70g) of sugar. Beat on low speed until smooth. Add the egg yolks and mix just to combine. Set the bowl over the simmering water. Beat on medium-high speed until the mixture is dark yellow and starting to resemble a custard, about 5 minutes. Off the water, continue beating to lower the temperature of the zabaglione to room temperature, about 4 minutes more. The zabaglione will continue to thicken as it cools.

4. Fold the lemon and orange zests into the zabaglione. Gently fold the meringue into the zabaglione, followed by the whipped cream. Don't overmix!

5. Line a 9 by 5-inch (23 by 13cm) loaf pan with plastic wrap, leaving 4 inches (10cm) of extra plastic hanging over the long sides of the pan. Pour the mixture into the pan and smooth the top with an offset spatula. Cover the top with the extra plastic. Freeze for at least 5 hours but ideally overnight.

6. Use the plastic to lift and invert the semifreddo onto a serving plate. Remove the plastic, cut into slices, and serve.

No-Churn Peanut Butter Curry Ice Cream

Makes 1½ quarts (1.4L) | From Cristina Sciarra

1 (14-ounce/397g)
can sweetened
condensed milk

¼ cup (25g) powdered
peanut butter

¼ cup (20g) skim
milk powder

1 tablespoon curry
powder

1 teaspoon vanilla extract

2 cups (475ml) heavy
cream, well chilled

Peanut butter takes a romp to the sleeker side with this ice cream that's stripped of eggs, an ice cream maker, and—gasp!—chocolate. Instead, the peanut butter mixture is sweetened just a little by condensed milk and spiced by curry powder and powdered peanut butter. If the words *powdered peanut butter* sound like molecular gastronomy, don't flip the page just yet. It's simply ground-up roasted peanuts, so the peanut flavor is super-pronounced. You can find it at your grocery store next to the usual jarred stuff or online—or whiz up your own. Blitz roasted unsalted peanuts in a food processor until the mixture resembles cornmeal, about 30 seconds.

If you think you'll miss peanut butter's sweeter side, top the ice cream with cayenne-spiced peanut brittle (page 50), flambéed bananas (page 125), toasted coconut flakes, or caramel sauce (page 85)—or take a cue from those PB&Js and drizzle on some warm compote (page 143).

1. Pour the condensed milk into a large bowl. Stir in the powdered peanut butter, milk powder, curry powder, and vanilla until combined.

2. In a large bowl, beat the heavy cream on medium-high speed until stiff peaks form, 5 to 7 minutes.

3. Mix a few spoonfuls of the whipped cream into the condensed milk mixture. Then fold in the remaining whipped cream until fully incorporated. Don't overmix.

4. Spoon the mixture into a container and freeze for at least 5 hours.

How to Make Ice Cream Without a Maker

Take the building blocks of this recipe to dream up other no-churn flavors: Mix 1 (14-ounce/397g) can of sweetened condensed milk in a large bowl with your flavor of choice. It's best if the flavor is in liquid form—heavy solids will weigh down this light-as-air ice cream. Say 1 to 2 tablespoons of vanilla or almond or peppermint extract, the same amount of rose or orange blossom water, or ½ cup (160g) of jam or ½ cup (120ml) of cold-brew coffee. Taste the mixture; if the flavor's faint, add more. Beat 2 cups (475ml) of chilled heavy cream and combine with the condensed milk mixture as directed.

Cayenne-Spiced Peanut Brittle

Makes 1 sheet pan of brittle | From Cristina Sciarra

2 cups (400g) sugar

¾ cup (175ml) light corn syrup

½ teaspoon kosher salt

3 cups (440g) skinless roasted salted peanuts

2 tablespoons unsalted butter

1 teaspoon cayenne pepper

1 teaspoon vanilla extract

2 teaspoons baking soda

Whereas many brittles are all-around sweet, this one has a sneaky heat that travels in small doses..To turn the big chunks (good for a gift) into a dust (for ice cream!), just cover the cooled brittle with parchment paper and use the heel of a large mug or a meat pounder to pulverize it—or pulse it in the food processor. Top or swirl the dust into creamy, warming flavors, like as shown on page 49, or apple–bay leaf ice cream (page 107), olive oil–cacao nib gelato (page 10), horchata ice cream (page 108), marzipan semifreddo (page 47), or carrot cake ice cream (page 103).

1. Line a large baking sheet with parchment paper, coat with cooking spray, and set aside.

2. In a large, heavy saucepan with high sides, whisk together the sugar, corn syrup, salt, and 1 cup (240ml) water. Boil over medium-high heat and cook, stirring every once in a while, until the mixture turns light brown, about 30 minutes. Stir in the peanuts and continue to cook, stirring semi-continuously, until the mixture reaches 275°F (135°C) on a candy thermometer, about 30 minutes more. Remove from the heat and stir in the butter, cayenne, and vanilla until combined. Stir in the baking soda and continue stirring for 10 to 15 seconds more.

3. Working quickly, pour the mixture onto the prepared baking sheet, using a heatproof spatula to scrape it all from the pan. Spread the brittle into a thin layer. Let the brittle cool completely on the baking sheet, about 40 minutes. When the brittle is hard, cut it into uneven chunks.

4. Store in an airtight container at room temperature for up to 3 weeks.

Salted Maple Honeycomb Candy

Makes 1 sheet pan of candy | From Merrill Stubbs

1¼ cups (250g) sugar

½ cup (120ml) maple syrup

1 tablespoon baking soda

1½ teaspoons flaky sea salt, like Maldon

Merrill calls this recipe—inspired by a popcorn ice cream with maple candy from Blue Marble in Brooklyn—a miracle of science. That's because adding a little baking soda to a dark maple caramel will give you an impossibly crunchy, airy candy. (Baking soda's the reason why your cakes and pancakes are pillowy, too.) We're happy Merrill's kind of science results in taste tests—ones we can break up into pieces to swirl into an ice cream just before it's done churning. Malted vanilla (page 23), peanut butter (page 48), fig (page 76), and butternut squash–tahini (page 150) are all flavors that'd be happy to have this candy whirled in. For an even richer treat, dip the candy pieces in melted semisweet chocolate and let them cool before adding to ice cream.

1. Line a large baking sheet with a silicone baking mat or greased parchment paper.

2. In a heavy saucepan, combine the sugar, maple syrup, and ¼ cup (60ml) cold water and cook over medium-high heat, stirring constantly, just until the sugar dissolves. Do not stir after the sugar dissolves, though you can swirl the pan occasionally if you'd like. Let the mixture come to a boil and continue to cook until it reaches 300°F (150°C) on a candy thermometer and is a dark amber color, 5 to 7 minutes.

3. Working quickly, remove from the heat and whisk in the baking soda just until incorporated. Immediately pour the mixture onto the prepared baking sheet, using a heatproof spatula to scrape it all from the pan. Do not smooth out the mixture—you'll get rid of all those air bubbles!

4. Still working quickly, evenly sprinkle the surface of the candy with the salt. Let the candy cool completely on the baking sheet. When the candy is hard, break it apart into uneven chunks with your fingers.

5. Store in an airtight container at room temperature for up to a week.

Chocolate-Hazelnut Baked Alaska

Serves 10 to 12 | From Cristina Sciarra, Posie Harwood, and Yossy Arefi

Chocolate-Hazelnut Ice Cream

1 tablespoon espresso powder

2 tablespoons boiling water or hot brewed coffee

½ cup (150g) chocolate-hazelnut spread

3½ ounces (100g) dark chocolate (70% cacao), chopped

1 (14-ounce/397g) can sweetened condensed milk

1 teaspoon vanilla extract

3 cups (710ml) heavy cream, well chilled

Cake

1 cup (200g) sugar

¾ cup plus 2 tablespoons (110g) all-purpose flour

6 tablespoons (35g) unsweetened cocoa powder

Scant 1 teaspoon baking powder

Scant 1 teaspoon baking soda

½ teaspoon kosher salt

½ cup (120ml) whole milk

1 egg

2 tablespoons vegetable oil

1 teaspoon vanilla extract

2 tablespoons boiling water or hot brewed coffee

If your mind wanders to images of tame, 1950s cocktail parties when you hear the words *Baked Alaska*, don't let it. Because—and let's pause here for a quick moment of adoration—would you look at this beautiful thing? She's a thoroughly modern mash-up of recipes from Food52 contributors—there's chocolate (Posie Harwood's cake) on chocolate (a take on Yossy Arefi's airy meringue), with coffee and hazelnut in Cristina Sciarra's no-churn ice cream.

You can make components ahead—the ice cream, the cake, even the meringue—and, on assembly, use either the oven or a kitchen torch to brown (crown?) the meringue. This is a scene-stealer, but not a fussy one. Thanks to sheer size, it'll stay pretty and frozen long after it comes out of the freezer.

1. To make the ice cream, stir together the espresso powder and boiling water and let sit for 2 minutes. Melt the chocolate-hazelnut spread and chocolate in the microwave in 15-second intervals, stirring between each.

2. Pour the condensed milk into a separate bowl. Whisk in the chocolate mixture, then the espresso and vanilla. Let cool for about 30 minutes.

3. In a large bowl, using a handheld electric mixer, whisk the heavy cream on medium-high speed until soft peaks form, 6 to 7 minutes. Stir a couple spoonfuls of the whipped cream into the condensed milk mixture. Then fold in the remaining whipped cream. Don't overmix.

4. Line a deep bowl that's about 8 inches (20cm) wide with plastic wrap, leaving extra plastic hanging over the edge. Pour the ice cream base into the bowl and cover the top with the overhanging plastic. Freeze for at least 6 hours but ideally overnight.

5. To make the cake, heat the oven to 350°F (175°C). Grease and flour a 9-inch (23cm) cake pan and line with parchment paper.

6. In a large bowl, whisk together the sugar, flour, cocoa powder, baking powder, baking soda, and salt. Beat in the milk, egg, vegetable oil, and vanilla. Beat the boiling water in just to incorporate.

CONTINUED

Meringue

5 egg whites

1¼ cups (250g) sugar

⅛ teaspoon kosher salt

3 tablespoons unsweetened cocoa powder

7. Pour the batter into the prepared pan. Bake until a toothpick inserted into the center comes out clean, 30 to 35 minutes. Let the cake cool for 15 minutes, then invert it onto a wire rack. Remove the parchment and let cool completely. (To make ahead, wrap the cake in plastic and store for up to 1 day at room temperature, up to 2 days in the refrigerator, and up to 2 weeks in the freezer.)

8. To make the meringue, fill a pot with 1½ inches (4cm) of water and bring to a simmer. In a heatproof bowl, combine the egg whites and sugar and set the bowl on top of the simmering water. Using a handheld electric mixer, beat the mixture on medium-high speed until white, opaque, and foamy, about 4 minutes. Off the water, continue mixing until the meringue is stiff and glossy, about 5 minutes more. Fold in the salt and cocoa powder just until combined.

9. Heat the oven to 450°F (230°C) or get a kitchen torch ready. Place the cake on a parchment-lined baking sheet. Trim the cake to the size of the top of your ice cream bowl. (The trimmings are the baker's treat.) Remove the plastic from the wide bottom of the ice cream, place your hand in the center, and invert the ice cream bowl onto the cake (the round side should be up). Remove the bowl but leave the plastic. Place the stacked cake and ice cream in the freezer while you prepare (mentally) for the next step.

10. You're almost to your baked Alaska! Make sure your meringue, torch (if using), and an offset spatula or spoon are near. Remove the plastic from the ice cream, then, working quickly, use the spatula or the back of the spoon to cover the cake and ice cream completely with the meringue. Consider pulling the meringue away from the cake to get little spikes, or massaging the meringue in circular motions to swoops and swirls. Bake for 3 minutes or use the kitchen torch to brown the meringue all over. If you need to pause at any time, you can return the cake to the freezer.

11. Serve immediately, or freeze, covered, for up to 2 weeks.

Fruity

Cherry Snow Cone

Serves 1 | From Liz Larkin

½ cup (75g) pitted
fresh sweet cherries

1 to 2 tablespoons
turbinado sugar

Torn leaves from
a mint sprig

1 teaspoon freshly
squeezed lemon juice
or orange juice

½ to 1 tablespoon
Pernod

1 cup (5g) ice cubes

1 tablespoon heavy
cream (optional)

This snow cone is sure to elicit as much joy as the one glommed all over your eight-year-old chin—albeit in a more adult, balanced form. It's still got an icy-crunchiness that relaxes into a cold, sticky drink, but here, there's muddled fruit and mint. The splash of anise-flavored Pernod makes it almost passable as a very tame cocktail, but the optional-but-not-really cream takes it from drink to dessert.

Feel free to make this with other stone fruit, or even berries, and change up the alcohol accordingly (Liz recommends kirsch; we're thinking amaro). To serve a crowd, keep pulverized ice in the freezer. It'll get a little slushy and melty, but remember, that sweet, syrupy pool at the bottom of the cup is the best part anyways.

1. Muddle the cherries, sugar, mint, lemon juice, and Pernod until you have a nice amount of syrup.

2. Finely crush or shave the ice in your trusty blender—or the snow cone machine that's been sitting in the closet for years. Working quickly, spoon the crushed ice into a bowl, ideally a transparent one so you can see all the dripping cherry goodness in about 30 seconds.

3. Pour the muddled cherry mixture, chunks and all, over the ice. Pour the heavy cream over the top. Add a straw and a spoon and have at it.

How to Pit a Cherry Without a Unitasking Contraption

The messy, wild way to pit cherries is by smashing them with the side of a chef's knife (see previous spread). But with an empty beer bottle and a chopstick, there's a cleaner, more contained way: Gently hold the cherry atop the (cleaned) beer bottle. Press the chopstick through the cherry to push the pit out the other side. The bottle collects the pits, keeping the whole process nice and neat. Bull's-eye, you could say.

Pineapple Breakfast Frozen Yogurt

Makes about 1 quart (950ml) | Adapted from Emily Vikre

1 cup (165g) pineapple chunks, cut into ½-inch (1.3cm) pieces

½ cup (120ml) maple syrup or ½ cup (100g) sugar

½ cup (120ml) heavy cream

⅓ cup (110g) honey

2 sprigs thyme (optional)

2 cups (475ml) full-fat plain Greek yogurt

1 teaspoon vanilla extract

When summer reaches the blistering point, even breakfast is better off frozen. Here, layers of frozen Greek yogurt cuddle with pineapple chunks, sticky and saucy from a simmer in maple syrup (Emily also does this to raspberries and plums.) The yogurt is rich for yogurt, drunk on honey and thyme, and relaxed from cream to keep it from freezing solid. Make it for breakfast, make it for dinner (you know you would)—or double the recipe and stow it in the freezer for a week of make-ahead morning meals. Granola and sunglasses optional.

1. In a small, heavy saucepan, boil the pineapple and maple syrup, then turn the heat to low and cook, uncovered, until the fruit breaks down, about 20 minutes. Remove from the heat and let cool completely. (For a smoother frozen yogurt, puree the mixture and pass it through a fine-mesh sieve.)

2. In a separate saucepan, bring the heavy cream and honey just to a boil, stirring to dissolve the honey, then remove from the heat and add the thyme sprigs. Let steep for 30 minutes, then discard the thyme. If you're not using the thyme, just warm the cream enough to dissolve the honey.

3. In a bowl, stir together the cream mixture, yogurt, and vanilla. Chill completely in the refrigerator, at least 2 hours but ideally overnight.

4. Pour the chilled base into an ice cream maker and churn it according to the manufacturer's instructions.

5. Spoon the frozen yogurt into a plastic container, layering it with spoonfuls of pineapple sauce, and freeze.

Shelf Life

One of the main reasons we all make ice cream is because fresh churns are amazingly soft, nearly bouncing out of the maker. After a day or two in the freezer—or a week for leaner ice creams, like sorbet—most homemade ice creams start to harden and lose their supple texture and flavor; they don't have the stabilizers of store-bought ice cream. It won't be bad, or go bad, but it won't be as good as on day one. To improve your ice creams' shelf life, try not to expose them to air very frequently (air makes ice crystals). When you're pulling ice cream from the freezer, let it soften for a few minutes before scooping. And if you think your homemade ice cream is beyond repair, just re-churn it (page 140)!

Lemony, Coconutty Raspberry Ice Cream Sandwiches

Makes about 24 ice cream sandwiches | From Emily Vikre

Raspberry Ice Cream

5 egg yolks

1½ cups (355ml) heavy cream

1½ cups (355ml) half-and-half

1 cup (200g) sugar

½ vanilla bean, split lengthwise

3 cups (710ml) strained raspberry puree (made from blending and straining about 30 ounces/850g fresh or frozen and defrosted raspberries)

1 tablespoon Chambord or crème de cassis (optional)

Coconut-Lemon Shortbread

1½ cups (340g) good-quality unsalted butter, softened

1 cup (200g) sugar

1 teaspoon sea salt

1 teaspoon freshly squeezed lemon juice

2⅔ cups (335g) all-purpose flour

1 cup (80g) toasted unsweetened finely shredded coconut

Grated zest of 2 lemons

Had Food52 community member and contributor Emily Vikre given us this coconut-lemon shortbread—light and crisp, tropical without being sunscreen-y—it would have been enough. Had she given us this raspberry ice cream—good with raspberries either fresh *or* frozen—it would have been enough. But no, she combined these stand-up desserts into two-bite ice cream sandwiches that are just plain adorable. The cookies are sandwich-perfect because they don't become stone-hard when frozen. For a shortcut, keep a batch of them in the freezer and turn them into sandwiches with store-bought ice cream (lemon sorbet would be very good).

1. To make the ice cream, lightly beat the egg yolks in a medium bowl. In a medium saucepan, bring the heavy cream, half-and-half, sugar, and vanilla seeds and pod to a simmer over medium-low heat.

2. Add about ¼ cup (60ml) of the cream mixture to the egg yolks, whisking furiously to temper the yolks. Add another ½ cup (120ml), continuing to whisk. Then scrape the egg mixture into the pan and simmer, stirring constantly, over low heat, until the custard thickens enough to coat the back of a spoon.

3. Pass the custard through a fine-mesh sieve into a large bowl. Stir in the raspberry puree and Chambord. Cover and chill completely for at least 4 hours but ideally overnight.

4. Pour the chilled custard into an ice cream maker and churn it according to the manufacturer's instructions. Spoon the ice cream into a container and freeze.

5. To make the shortbread, using a stand mixer fitted with the paddle attachment, beat the butter and sugar on medium-high speed until light and fluffy, 5 to 7 minutes. Beat in the salt and lemon juice.

6. Beat in half of the flour just until combined. Add the remaining flour, the toasted coconut, and the lemon zest and continue to beat just until the dough pulls away from the sides of the bowl and almost forms a single mass, about 2 minutes.

CONTINUED

7. Gather the dough together, flatten it into a disc, cover with plastic wrap, and chill for about 1 hour.

8. Heat your oven to 325°F (165°C). Line 2 baking sheets with parchment paper. On a lightly floured surface, roll out the dough until it's about ¼ inch (6mm) thick. Using a 2-inch (5cm) round cookie cutter, cut out as many cookies as possible and place on the prepared baking sheets. Gather the scraps, roll out the dough again, and cut out more cookies, using as little flour as possible all the while. Continue until you've used up all of the dough. Bake, rotating the baking sheets halfway through, until the cookies are golden brown, 16 to 20 minutes. Keep uncooked cookies in the fridge while they wait their turn.

9. Let the cookies cool on the baking sheet for about 3 minutes, then transfer to a wire rack to cool completely.

10. Let the ice cream soften for a few minutes before scooping. Place a scoop of ice cream on the flat side of a cookie. Cover with another cookie, flat side down, and press gently. Continue until all of the cookies are gone (or all of the ice cream, whichever comes first, but the amounts should be fairly well matched). Cover with plastic wrap and transfer to the freezer as you go.

11. Either eat right away, or keep in the freezer for just the right moment.

Strawberry, Hazelnut & Maple Waffle Sandwiches

Makes 1 quart (950ml) ice cream—the number of sandwiches depends on waffle size | From Cristina Sciarra

Strawberry-Hazelnut Ice Cream

1 pound (450g) hulled strawberries

½ cup (120ml) pure maple syrup

1 teaspoon olive oil

⅛ teaspoon kosher salt

2 cups (475ml) heavy cream

1 cup (240ml) whole milk

½ cup (35g) skim milk powder

¼ cup (50g) sugar

4 egg yolks

⅔ cup (90g) crushed toasted hazelnuts

Your favorite waffle recipe (yeasted taste great here)

Before you go thinking we just smooshed plain ol' strawberry ice cream between two toaster waffles, read on—because the strawberry flavor is subtle and mature, the result of fruit roasted with maple syrup. And the waffle is any you love, sweetened by maple and hazelnuts, though you could certainly use ones from your freezer. If you make the sandwiches in advance and freeze them, the waffle will sag just a bit. The other option is reserved for thrill-seekers: Waffle, hot—ice cream, quickly melting.

1. Heat the oven to 425°F (220°C). Combine the strawberries, maple syrup, olive oil, and salt on a parchment-lined baking sheet. Toss until the strawberries are evenly coated. Roast the strawberries until they are shrunken, juicy, and bubbling, about 20 minutes. (Work quickly as you complete the next three steps, so that the "strawberry caramel" doesn't have time to set. If it does, simply pour some of the warm ice cream base onto the baking sheet and whisk to melt.)

2. Meanwhile, in a pot, whisk together the heavy cream, milk, milk powder, and 2 tablespoons of the sugar. Bring the mixture to a simmer over medium-low heat, then remove from the heat.

3. In a bowl, whisk the egg yolks with the remaining 2 tablespoons sugar for 1 minute. Gradually whisk the milk mixture into the yolks.

4. Pour the milk-yolk mix back into the pot and cook over medium-low heat, stirring occasionally, until the ice cream base thickens enough to coat the back of a spoon. Pass the mixture through a fine-mesh sieve set over a large bowl. Scrape every last drop of the strawberries into the bowl. Let the base steep for 30 minutes, then pass it through a fine-mesh sieve again; don't push the whole strawberries—set them aside. Chill the base and the strawberries separately in the refrigerator for at least 4 hours but ideally overnight.

5. Pour the chilled base into an ice cream maker and churn it according to the manufacturer's instructions. During the last 2 minutes of churning, add the chilled whole strawberries and about half of the hazelnuts.

CONTINUED

6. Spoon the ice cream into a container and freeze for at least 3 hours.

7. Make a batch of your favorite waffle recipe. To the batter, add the remaining hazelnuts (if you're using a yeasted recipe, add them right before you let the batter rest). Just before you're ready to cook the waffles, pour in ½ cup (120ml) maple syrup. After cooking, let the waffles cool on a wire rack for 10 minutes, then break apart or cut waffles into sandwich sizes.

8. Soften the ice cream before scooping. Place a large scoop of ice cream at the center of your waffle bottom. Top with a second waffle piece and press gently to smoosh the ice cream. Continue until all the waffles and ice cream are gone.

9. Eat immediately, or place the waffle sandwiches on a wire rack set on a baking sheet, cover with plastic wrap, and freeze.

Build a Better Sandwich

Sandwich making is an art, and frozen varieties are no different. The ice cream needs to be semi-firm so it's scoopable—not right out of the freezer (when it's too hard) or the machine (when it's too soft). While you can make a sandwich with any sort of ice cream, creamier ones—as opposed to, say, sorbet—have an easier time of getting to that soft yet not-too-melty sweet spot.

You want the cookies to be ready to bite into straight from the freezer; ones that are like brownies or shortbread (or *are* brownies or shortbread) work well. Other good ideas include croissants, pound cake, Rice Krispies treats, and meringues. Where crunchy veers problematic is if your cookie is too thin and will break at first bite, so if you must use your favorite crispy cookie, make them a little thicker. You can make sandwiches right when you want to eat them—the ice cream runs down your hands. If you like a sandwich that's more of a unit, put the sandwiches on a baking sheet, cover with plastic so the ice cream doesn't dry out, and freeze. Smart cookies plan ahead.

Blueberry Ice Cream

Makes about 1½ quarts (1.4L) | From Merrill Stubbs

1½ cups (355ml) whole milk

1½ cups (355ml) heavy cream

¾ cup (150g) sugar

4 egg yolks

1 vanilla bean, split lengthwise, or 1 teaspoon vanilla extract

2 cups (300g) blueberries, washed and picked over

The purest way to enjoy wild Maine blueberries is, according to our co-founder, covered with milk and showered lightly with sugar. But when she's had her fill of blueberry cereal, she turns to her creamy, airy blueberry ice cream. While Maine or any wild blueberries are preferred for maximum blueberry flavor, conventional or even frozen will work, too.

1. In a small saucepan, whisk together the milk, heavy cream, and ½ cup (100g) of the sugar. Cook over medium-low heat, stirring occasionally, until it reaches 175°F (80°C) on a candy thermometer.

2. Meanwhile, in a bowl, beat the egg yolks with the remaining ¼ cup (50g) sugar until pale yellow and thick. Gradually whisk a small amount of the milk mixture into the egg yolks. Whisk the thinned egg yolks back into the saucepan. Add the seeds from the vanilla bean.

3. Cook the custard over medium-low heat, stirring constantly, until it thickens enough to coat the back of a spoon (do *not* allow it to boil!). Pass the custard through a fine-mesh sieve into a large bowl. Chill the custard completely in the fridge, for at least 4 hours but ideally overnight.

4. Blend the cold custard and the blueberries until the berries are broken down, the mixture is violet in color, but a few small shreds of blueberry are still visible. Chill again for at least 2 hours.

5. Pour the chilled base into an ice cream maker and churn it according to the manufacturer's instructions.

Blueberry Graham Cracker Milkshake

Plop two scoops of softened blueberry ice cream per person into the blender (you could also use vanilla ice cream plus 1 cup/150g fresh or frozen blueberries). Add ½ cup (120ml) whole milk per person, blend, and test the thickness. If it's too thick, add more milk. If it's too thin, add more ice cream. Break one graham cracker per person into bite-size chunks and toss them into the blender. Blend and top with whipped cream.

Mango Lassicles

Makes 8 pops | From Nicholas Day

1½ cups (290g) fresh mango pulp (made by whirring ripe mango in the food processor or blender)

1 cup (240ml) full-fat plain Greek yogurt

1 tablespoon honey

Pinch of kosher salt

Pinch of ground cardamom

Mango, yogurt, a bare whisper of honey, and even barer whispers of salt and cardamom. That's all that goes into this recipe. The result is an ice pop that's pared down and pure—the same way a mango lassi is: cooling, zippy, and sweetly mango.

1. Blend all of the ingredients very well until smooth.

2. Pour the mixture into the pop molds, dividing it evenly. Freeze for at least 4 hours, or overnight. Then lick.

Genius Tip: Frozen Yogurt, Straight Up

Once you realize, thanks to Max Falkowitz and Ethan Frisch from Serious Eats, that the best frozen yogurt takes only three ingredients to make, will you ever set foot in one of those self-serve shops again? Simply whisk together 4 cups (950ml) of full-fat plain yogurt, 1 cup (200g) of sugar (you read that right—sugar is what keeps the fro-yo soft and scoopable), and ¼ teaspoon of kosher salt until the sugar dissolves. Chill the mixture in the refrigerator until it's thoroughly chilled. Pour it into an ice cream maker and churn it according to the manufacturer's instructions. Serve it straight from the machine, like soft serve, or spoon it into an airtight container and freeze for 4 hours to scoop it like ice cream. Whether you choose to charge friends by weight is also up to you.

Genius Tip: Peel a Mango Easy-Peasy

Katie Quinn, a video journalist and food writer, found the simplest way to peel a mango—and all you need is a drinking glass. Cut the mango along the pit in the center (as you normally do). Take one piece and find where the skin meets the flesh at the south pole of the fruit. Align that part with the edge of the glass and push the glass along the fruit, keeping the skin outside the glass and the flesh on the inside. Repeat with the other side. Peeled mango!

Grilled Watermelon Cremolada with Honey & Lime

Serves 6 to 8 | From Cristina Sciarra

5 tablespoons (100g) honey

¾ cup (175ml) freshly squeezed lime juice

1 small seedless watermelon, ends trimmed, cut crosswise into 1-inch (2.5cm) slices

¼ cup (50g) turbinado sugar

A cremolada is Peru's jaunty take on a slushy—and the frosty dessert-drink you always hoped your big-batch piña coladas would become as they sweltered in the sunshine. Here, the melt is intentional and the method is breezy: Blend tropical fruit juice with sugar and water and freeze in ice cube trays; when frozen, blend again with a little more puree into a soft slurry. Because the base lives in the freezer, you can double or triple the recipe ahead of time and then mix together individual drinks for friends throughout your shindig.

We want to try cremoladas with cantaloupe, mango, tamarind, banana, papaya, pomegranate, strawberry, and pineapple. (Start with 3½ pounds/1.5kg of chopped fruit and go from there.) If we want to frill, fresh herbs will make an appearance at the second blend—tequila or gin, too.

1. In a small bowl, whisk a tablespoon of the honey with ¼ cup (60ml) of the lime juice. Brush both sides of each watermelon slice with the lime mixture.

2. Heat a grill (or grill pan) to medium-high heat. Grill the watermelon slices until grill marks appear, 4 to 5 minutes per side, basting as you go. Let cool to room temperature, about 5 minutes. Cut and discard the rind.

3. Blend the watermelon, remaining ¼ cup (85g) honey, ½ cup (115ml) lime juice, the sugar, and ½ cup (120ml) water until smooth, about a minute. (Process in batches if necessary.) Pass the mixture through a fine-mesh sieve into a large bowl. (You should have about 8 cups/1.9L of watermelon puree.) Refrigerate 2½ cups (590ml) of the puree until cool. Pour the remaining puree into ice cube trays and freeze until solid, at least 5 hours.

4. Blend the watermelon cubes, then pour in the cold puree and blend until thick and slushy, about 2 minutes. Add up to ½ cup (120ml) water to get the right consistency.

5. Divide among 6 to 8 tall glasses. Serve right away with tall spoons and straws.

Roasted Peaches with Lemon Spoom

Serves 6 to 12; makes 1 quart (950ml) spoom | From Cristina Sciarra

6 small to medium
peaches, halved
and pitted

6 tablespoons (85g)
unsalted butter

¼ cup (55g) packed
light brown sugar

4 small lemons, halved

1¼ cups (250g)
granulated sugar

3 egg whites

¼ teaspoon
cream of tartar

⅛ teaspoon kosher salt

1 teaspoon vanilla extract

Dress sorbet in satin and you'll have spoom. Its funny name comes from
spuma, the Italian word for "foam"—a fitting description for its frothy texture
that comes from the meringue that serves as its base.

Here, you flavor that shiny meringue with a roasted-lemon syrup, churn
it like you would regular ice cream, then serve it right away (or, if you must,
freeze it for 3 to 4 hours). Spoon the spoom—luxe, light, and elegant—over
slumped roasted peaches, with a little Prosecco poured over if you feel like it
(or you're on summer vacation, or a European getaway).

1. Heat the oven to 425°F (220°C). Nestle the peaches in a baking dish, cut side
up. In a small pot over medium-low heat, melt the butter with the brown sugar,
whisking occasionally until the sugar dissolves. Pour over the peaches, then add
the halved lemons, cut sides up. Bake for 50 minutes, until the peaches start to
slump. (You can store the peaches and the lemons separately in the refrigerator
for up to a day.)

2. In a pot, cook 1 cup (240ml) water and ½ cup (100g) of the granulated sugar
over low heat, whisking occasionally, until the sugar dissolves. Remove from
the heat. Juice the roasted lemons and stir ½ cup (120ml) of juice into the
sugar syrup. Refrigerate the syrup for at least 2 hours, or up to 2 days.

3. Simmer a medium pot with 1½ inches (4cm) of water. In a large heatproof
bowl, combine the remaining ¾ cup (150g) of granulated sugar, egg whites,
and cream of tartar and set the bowl on top of the simmering water. Beat
the mixture on medium-high speed until shiny and opaque, 3 to 4 minutes.
Remove the bowl from the simmering water and continue mixing until
the meringue is stiff and glossy, about 5 minutes more. Fold in the salt and
vanilla. Fold the lemon syrup into the meringue until fully incorporated.

4. Pour the base into an ice cream maker and churn it according to the
manufacturer's instructions.

5. Serve the spoom straight from the machine, like soft serve, or spoon into
a container and freeze for 3 to 4 hours.

6. Rewarm the peaches in a small saucepan over low heat. Divide the peaches
and their juices among 6 to 12 tall glasses and scoop the spoom on top.

Fig Ice Cream with Chocolate Swirl & Marcona Almonds

Makes about 1 quart (950ml) | From Cristina Sciarra

Caramelized Figs

Packed 1 cup (200g) dried or fresh Turkish, California, or Black Mission figs

2 tablespoons unsalted butter

2 tablespoons dark brown sugar

Ice Cream

2 cups (475ml) heavy cream

1 cup (240ml) whole milk

½ cup (35g) skim milk powder

5 tablespoons (60g) granulated sugar

¼ cup (50g) packed light brown sugar

4 egg yolks

¼ cup (35g) chopped Marcona almonds

Chocolate Swirl

3 ounces (85g) dark chocolate (70% cacao), broken into pieces

1 tablespoon solid coconut oil

Instead of a bite of dried fig here or a swirl of jam there, every spoonful of this ice cream is intensely jammy, like biting into the ripe fruit, but cushioned by soft cream. With a ribbon of dark chocolate acting as a foil to the fruity sweetness and silky, salty, creamy Marcona almonds, you've made a heavenly ice cream version of a chocolate-dipped, nut-coated fig.

1. If you're using dried figs, let the figs sit in 2 cups (475ml) boiling water until plump, about 20 minutes. Drain, then transfer the figs to a saucepan, along with the butter, brown sugar, and ½ cup (120ml) room-temperature water. Cook over medium heat until the figs are soft and jammy, about 15 minutes. If you're using fresh figs, trim the ends and cook them with the butter, brown sugar, and room-temperature water until soft and jammy, closer to 10 minutes.

2. To make the ice cream, in a pot, whisk together the heavy cream, milk, milk powder, ¼ cup (50g) of the granulated sugar, and the brown sugar. Bring to a simmer over medium-low heat, then remove from the heat.

3. Whisk together the egg yolks with the remaining 1 tablespoon sugar for 30 seconds. Gradually whisk the milk mixture into the yolks.

4. Pour the milk-yolk mixture back into the pot and cook over medium-low heat, stirring occasionally, until the ice cream base thickens enough to coat the back of a spoon.

5. Pass the base through a fine-mesh sieve into a large bowl. Add the fig compote and blend until smooth, 1 to 2 minutes. Let the warm base steep for 30 minutes. Chill the base completely in the refrigerator for at least 4 hours but ideally overnight.

6. Pour the chilled base into an ice cream maker and churn it according to the manufacturer's instructions. During the last minute of churning, add the almonds.

7. While the ice cream is churning, melt the chocolate and coconut oil in the microwave. Let the chocolate cool, about 10 minutes.

8. Using a spoon, Jackson Pollock one-third of the chocolate swirl into a plastic container, followed by one-third of the ice cream. Repeat two more times, reserving some of the chocolate to drizzle on top. Freeze for at least 4 hours.

Bourbon Prune Velvet

Makes about 7 cups (1.7L) | From Amanda Hesser

1 cup (175g) chopped plump prunes

⅓ cup (80ml) bourbon or dark rum

¾ cup (150g) sugar

3 egg whites, at room temperature

Pinch of kosher salt

2 cups (475ml) heavy cream

A velvet is an old way of making ice cream before ice cream machines were more the norm. The word *velvet* comes from the beautifully supple texture of the meringue-based ice cream.

When you see the words *candy thermometer*, please don't turn the page. If you haven't yet bought one, this is the moment. And as long as you have a mixer or immersion blender, this six-ingredient recipe is way easier than making cookies.

1. Place the prunes and bourbon in a small bowl and let macerate while you work on other components.

2. In a small saucepan, combine the sugar and ¼ cup (60ml) water and attach a candy thermometer to the pan. Set over high heat and bring to a boil to dissolve the sugar. Turn the heat to medium-low and cook until the syrup reaches 236°F (113°C), or soft-ball stage.

3. Meanwhile, in a stand mixer fitted with the whisk attachment, beat the egg whites and salt on high speed until stiff peaks form, 3 to 5 minutes. When the syrup is ready, keep the mixer going and pour the syrup into the egg whites in a thin stream. Now you have meringue—keep beating it until it forms stiff peaks again. Put the mixer bowl in the fridge and chill the meringue for about 30 minutes.

4. Whip the heavy cream on high speed until soft peaks form, 2 to 3 minutes. Fold the prunes and bourbon into the cold meringue, followed by the whipped cream. Spoon the velvet into a container and freeze for up to a week.

Genius Tip: With Olive Oil on Top

To avoid a cloying ice cream and bring out savoriness, drizzle good-quality extra-virgin olive oil and sprinkle flaky sea salt over your ice cream. Big Gay Ice Cream in New York City serves vanilla ice cream with fig sauce, toasted pine nuts, olive oil, and sea salt.

Fizzy Orange Sherbet Coolers

Makes about 1 quart (950ml) sherbet and, in turn, many coolers | From Emily Connor

Orange Sherbet

1 cup (200g) sugar

1 tablespoon grated orange or lemon zest

⅛ teaspoon kosher salt

2 cups (475ml) orange juice, preferably freshly squeezed

¼ cup (60ml) freshly squeezed lemon juice

⅔ cup (160ml) heavy cream

For Each Cooler

½ cup (120ml) orange juice, preferably freshly squeezed, chilled

½ cup (120ml) seltzer, chilled

1 to 2 scoops orange sherbet

By churning airy whipped cream with freshly squeezed orange juice, you'll get a silky-smooth sherbet that's refreshing enough to eat on its own. But not so fast! Blend those scoops with seltzer and more orange juice for a drink that's velvety like a Creamsicle but with the tart fizz of Orangina.

1. To make the sherbet, in a food processor, pulse the sugar, orange zest, and salt until the sugar is fragrant, 10 to 15 times. With the processor running, add the orange and lemon juices and process until the sugar dissolves, about 1 minute.

2. Pass the mixture through a fine-mesh sieve into a bowl. Cover the bowl with plastic wrap and chill in the freezer until very cold but not frozen, about 45 minutes, or in the refrigerator for at least 2 hours.

3. In a large bowl, beat the heavy cream on high speed until soft peaks form, 2 to 3 minutes. With the mixer running, slowly pour the cold juice mixture into the whipped cream so that the stream hits the side of the bowl.

4. Pour the sherbet base into an ice cream maker and churn it according to the manufacturer's instructions.

5. Spoon the sherbet into a container and freeze until firm, about 3 hours.

6. To assemble a cooler, pour the orange juice and seltzer into a tall glass, leaving enough room for the sherbet. Add the sherbet and let it fizz. Repeat till you get the desired number of coolers. Alternatively, blend the 3 ingredients together for a shake of sorts.

Do the Dairy Flip-Flop

Poke around this book and you'll see a whole lot of heavy cream and whole milk, but they're in different quantities. That's because dairy—as much as fruit or vanilla extract—is a flavor in your ice cream, in addition to making your finished product, you know, creamy. So you can slide the ratios of cream to milk around to suit the ice cream you're after. If you want an ice cream that's more fruity, take the fat down—leaner mixtures make other flavors pop. The worst thing that can happen is the ice cream will turn up a different consistency, but as Alice Medrich puts it, "Where is this great fear of iciness? Richer and creamier isn't always better."

Herbs & Spices

Lemongrass Chile Ginger Ice Cream

Makes about 2½ quarts (2.4L) | From Derek Laughren

5 cups (1.2L) heavy cream

2½ cups (590ml) whole milk

1½ cups (300g) sugar

½ teaspoon kosher salt

8 ounces (225g) fresh ginger, peeled and sliced thinly

2 stalks lemongrass, trimmed, cut into 2-inch (5cm) lengths, and crushed with the back of a knife

4 Thai bird chiles, halved (do not remove seeds or ribs)

12 egg yolks

1 cup (150g) crystallized ginger, finely chopped (optional)

Sure, this ice cream is surprising—it's savory curry in ice cream form: earthy lemongrass, ginger, heat. But the flavors are in just the right balance so that they end up exciting instead of unexpected for the sake of being different. Derek, our former test kitchen manager, gives "bonus points if you make yourself a float with good, dry ginger beer."

1. In a saucepan, whisk together the heavy cream, milk, 1 cup (200g) of the sugar, and the salt. Add the fresh ginger, lemongrass, and chiles and cook over medium-low heat, stirring frequently, until just simmering. Off the heat, cover and let steep for 30 minutes.

2. Blend the mixture until it's as smooth as you can get it (you may need to work in batches). Pass through a fine-mesh sieve into a bowl and discard the solids.

3. Clean the saucepan and return the mixture to it. In a heatproof bowl, whisk your egg yolks. Whisk the remaining ½ cup (100g) of sugar into the yolks until it dissolves and the yolks are pale in color. Temper the eggs by gradually whisking in a few cups of the strained puree. Whisk the egg mixture into the saucepan.

4. Cook over medium-low heat, stirring constantly, until the mixture coats the back of a spoon.

5. Pass the ice cream base through a fine-mesh sieve into a bowl and chill completely in the refrigerator for at least 4 hours but ideally overnight.

6. Pour the chilled base into an ice cream maker and churn it according to the manufacturer's instructions. During the last minute of churning, add the crystallized ginger.

Miso Caramel

Like balsamic butterscotch (page 19), Kathy Wielech Patterson's miso caramel follows in the footsteps of salted caramel, confirming (again) that caramel + salt = great. To make a pint, in a heavy saucepan, bring ¾ cup (150g) sugar and ¼ cup (60ml) water to a boil over medium-high heat without stirring. When the sugar becomes a deep golden brown and wisps of smoke start to form, take it off the heat and carefully stir in ½ cup (120ml) heavy cream. If the caramel seizes up, put the pan back over low heat and stir until liquid again. Then, the zinger: Then whisk in 2 tablespoons of white miso (darker miso will be stronger). Let cool before refrigerating in an airtight container. Remelt the sauce in the microwave.

Mochi

Makes about 2 cups (220g) | From Cynthia Chen McTeman

1 cup (160g) sweet rice flour (mochiko), plus more for dusting

1 cup (200g) sugar

½ teaspoon baking powder

¾ cup (175ml) full-fat coconut milk

The tender chew of mochi—which you may think of as a bouncy topping for frozen yogurt or a chubby wrapper for a sphere of ice cream—comes from sweet glutinous rice. Traditionally, the grains are soaked, steamed, and then—in a feat of immense strength, coordination, and rhythm—pounded with heavy wooden mallets in a Japanese ceremony called *mochi-tsuki*.

But there's a shortcut: sweet rice *flour*. Buy a bag at an Asian grocery store (it's usually labeled as *mochiko*), then find the rest of the ingredients in your pantry. Whisk, bake, cool, and cut into softer, stickier gummy bear-like treats.

The recipe's creator suggests adding a tablespoon of rose water or a half teaspoon of almond or peppermint extract. Mix a teaspoon or two of matcha powder with the dry ingredients, or replace the water with Thai tea (and place atop a Thai tea snow cone, page 113, of course!).

1. Heat the oven to 275°F (135°C). Line a 9 by 13-inch (23 by 33cm) glass baking dish with parchment paper, leaving extra parchment hanging over the long sides of the pan. Butter the paper and stick the pan in the fridge.

2. In a large bowl, whisk together the rice flour, sugar, and baking powder. In a separate bowl, whisk together 1 cup (240ml) water and coconut milk. Whisk the wet ingredients into the dry ingredients.

3. Pour the mixture into the prepared baking dish. Cover loosely with aluminum foil. Bake for 1 hour—the mochi is done when it is soft and gelatinous but holds its shape when touched. (If you've already baked the mochi for an hour and it hasn't set, raise the temperature to 300°F/150°C and bake, uncovered, for 10 to 15 minutes more.) Let cool completely.

4. Dust a work surface with sweet rice flour. Lift the parchment and invert the mochi onto the dusted work surface. Remove the parchment paper and sprinkle rice flour over the mochi. Cover a knife blade in plastic wrap, then cut the mochi however you want; possibly bite-size pieces for topping or a couple of big squares for an ice cream dumpling. Dust the mochi pieces again with rice flour, transfer to an airtight container and store for up to 1 week in the fridge, or frozen for months. (Cynthia suggests trying them just slightly thawed right out of the freezer!)

Lavender–Coconut Milk Ice Cream

Makes about 1 quart (950ml) | From Cristina Sciarra

1 (14-ounce/400ml) can coconut cream

1 (14-ounce/400ml) can full-fat coconut milk

½ cup (100g) turbinado sugar

¼ cup (60ml) light corn syrup

Heaping 1 teaspoon tapioca starch

2 tablespoons edible dried lavender

1 tablespoon vodka

For those of you out there who find lavender ice cream soapy—or vegan ice cream icy—be prepared to eat your words (and more lavender–coconut milk ice cream, pictured on page ii). Coconut milk doesn't have enough fat to freeze up convincingly silky, but with a little help from coconut cream, it can churn into a very scoopable ice cream the texture of satin and the flavor of pure coconut (in addition to—not dominated by—lavender). You can find coconut cream at Asian groceries or online (or skim off the thick top of a chilled can of full-fat coconut milk). Be sure not to buy cream of coconut in its place; it's heavily sweetened and belongs in your piña colada.

1. In a pot, bring the coconut cream, coconut milk, sugar, corn syrup, and tapioca starch to a simmer over medium heat; the fat in the coconut milk and cream should start to "melt." Simmer, whisking occasionally, for 5 minutes. Blend with an immersion blender for 1 minute.

2. Off the heat, add the lavender and vodka. Let steep for 30 minutes. Pass the base through a fine-mesh sieve into a large bowl, then blend for 30 seconds. Chill the base completely in the refrigerator at least 5 hours but ideally overnight.

3. Pour the chilled base into an ice cream maker and churn it according to the manufacturer's instructions.

An Olive Branch to Corn Syrup

Corn syrup has an image problem—it's processed, it's not good for us, it's really sticky. Last time we checked, though, sugar wasn't the best thing for us either, and here we are, writing an ice cream book. Corn syrup is tap-dancing around this book because it helps ice cream melt slower, makes ice cream less icy, gives ice cream a good texture, but doesn't add any flavor like honey or agave might. It's especially needed in recipes that are low in fat, like sorbets, so the final product doesn't end up gritty. You will see recipes that have some corn syrup in addition to sugar—that's because using only corn syrup might mean diluted flavors (it's a liquid, and sugar just tastes better), a really dense consistency, and a humorously slow churn.

Basil-Shiso Castella Cake

Makes a 9-inch (23cm) cake (plus a loaf cake—chef's treat) | From Bobbi Lin

Basil-Shiso Gelato

2 cups (475ml) whole milk

1 cup (240ml) heavy cream

½ cup (100g) granulated sugar

¼ cup (50g) lightly packed light brown sugar

6 egg yolks

1½ cups (30g) loosely packed fresh basil leaves

½ cup (10g) loosely packed fresh shiso leaves

1 teaspoon grated lemon zest

Pinch of kosher salt

Castella Cake

¼ cup (60ml) whole milk

⅓ cup (110g) honey

7 eggs, at room temperature

1¼ cups (250g) granulated sugar

1½ cups (190g) bread flour, sifted

One sweltering summer Saturday, we were waiting for Bobbi, one of our photographers, at a barbecue. She was running late because she was figuring out how to affix her gelato cake to her bike—and keep it from melting as she rode over. "The cake is worth it," she justified, and since the party ended with us pesky editors asking for the recipe, you know she was right. Unlike other ice cream cakes, it's light and fresh more than creamy—and green (see it on the next page).

Now that you know a little about Bobbi, you won't be surprised to know that this was the first time she'd made this cake, combining two recipes she typically makes separately (as you could, too). The gelato, adapted from *Good Company* magazine, is spry with basil and basil's ruffled-edge Asian cousin shiso, which tastes like a more gingery mint. The cake is a classic Japanese sponge Bobbi adapted from the website Japanese Cooking 101. For even more flair, make it into two layers, add matcha to the cake, top with crumbled meringues made from the gelato's leftover egg whites, and/or bring the cake on a bike.

1. To make the gelato, in a saucepan, whisk together the milk, heavy cream, and both sugars. Bring to a boil, then immediately lower the heat and simmer, stirring until the sugar dissolves, about 5 minutes. Remove from the heat.

2. In a medium bowl, whisk together the egg yolks, then whisk in about a third of the milk mixture. Whisk the tempered yolks back into the milk mixture, until it thickens enough to coat the back of a spoon. Let cool.

3. Blend the basil, shiso, and ½ cup (120ml) of the milk-yolk mixture until smooth. Stir the herb puree into the milk-yolk mixture, followed by the lemon zest and salt.

4. Chill the base completely in the refrigerator for at least 4 hours but ideally overnight.

5. Pour the chilled base into an ice cream maker and churn it according to the manufacturer's instructions. Spoon into an airtight container and freeze. Makes a quart (950ml) of gelato.

CONTINUED

6. To make the cake, heat the oven to 350°F (175°C). Grease the bottom and sides of a 9-inch (23cm) springform pan and a loaf pan, line them with parchment paper, and grease again.

7. Microwave the milk and honey just until the honey melts, about 10 seconds.

8. Using a stand mixer fitted with the whisk attachment, beat the eggs on medium-high speed, adding the sugar in 3 additions, until the mixture triples in volume, about 7 minutes.

9. Turn the mixer speed to low and alternate adding the flour and the milk mixture in 4 total parts, beating after each until fully incorporated. Scrape down the sides of the bowl and fold gently.

10. Pour the batter into the prepared pans. Bake for 10 minutes, then lower the oven temperature to 320°F (160°C) and bake until a toothpick inserted into the centers comes out clean, 20 to 30 minutes for the loaf cake and 30 to 40 minutes for the springform. If the cakes are browning too soon, cover with aluminum foil.

11. Remove the cakes from the oven and immediately hold the springform pan about 5 inches (13cm) above a counter and drop it. This will release the air in the cake so it doesn't collapse. Take the cake out of the pan, remove the parchment, then transfer to a wire rack to cool. Let the loaf cake cool completely before turning out.

12. Soften the gelato until it's stirrable. Return the round cake to the springform pan. Spread the softened gelato evenly over the cake. Cover with plastic wrap and freeze for 1 hour.

13. Remove the sides of the springform pan, cut the cake into slices, and serve.

Cherry Sorbet with Lemon-Thyme Soda

Serves 6 | From Cristina Sciarra

Cherry Sorbet

4 1/2 cups (700g) frozen, pitted cherries

1/2 cup (100g) granulated sugar

1 tablespoon kirsch

1/8 teaspoon kosher salt

1 medium lemon, halved

2 tablespoons turbinado sugar

Lemon-Thyme Soda

2 cups (475ml) freshly squeezed lemon juice

1 cup (200g) granulated sugar

1 tablespoon grated lemon zest

6 sprigs thyme

Sparkling water, for topping

This tart twist on the cherry lime rickey puts the cherries in sorbet form, swaps lime for lemon, and tosses in a few sprigs of thyme for kicks. The key to the punchy cherry sorbet is roasting the fruit, which Cristina learned from another Food52 superstar, Emily Connor. Because this step really concentrates the cherry flavor, it works great with frozen cherries—save the fresh ones for snow cones (page 59).

1. To make the sorbet, heat the oven to 400°F (200°C). In a 9 by 13-inch (23 by 33cm) baking pan, toss together the cherries, granulated sugar, kirsch, and salt. Settle the cherries into a single layer. Nestle in the lemon halves, cut side up.

2. Bake until foamy and bubbling, about 30 minutes. Pour 1 cup (240ml) water into the pan and continue baking until the cherries have fallen apart, 15 minutes longer. Let the cherries cool, about 30 minutes.

3. Blend the cherries, their juices, and the turbinado sugar. Juice the lemon halves into the blender. Puree until smooth, about 1 minute. Chill the base completely for at least 4 hours but ideally overnight.

4. Pour the chilled base into an ice cream maker and churn it according to the manufacturer's instructions. Spoon the sorbet into a container and freeze until firm, at least 3 hours.

5. To make the syrup for the soda, in a pot, whisk together the lemon juice, granulated sugar, lemon zest, and 1/2 cup (120ml) water. Add the thyme and bring to a boil over medium heat. Lower the heat and simmer until thickened, about 40 minutes. Off the heat, let steep for 20 minutes. Strain the syrup through a fine-mesh sieve into a bowl and let cool. (Store in a sealed container in the refrigerator for up to 5 days.)

6. Divide the syrup among 6 glasses. Add a scoop of the sorbet. Top with sparkling water and serve with long spoons and straws.

Sgroppino

As with all age-old recipes, the iterations for this smooth-as-silk Venetian cocktail are endless, but the method with the most integrity, according to our Italian correspondent Emiko Davies, goes like this: Whisk softened lemon sorbet until it resembles frosting. Add an equal amount of Prosecco slowly, whisking until incorporated. Drink from fancy glasses: the sorbet supple, the bubbles still bubbling.

Mint-Basil Chip Ice Cream

Makes about 1 quart (950ml) | From Virginia Kellner

1 cup (240ml) whole milk

1 cup (20g) loosely packed mint leaves, torn

1 cup (20g) loosely packed basil leaves, torn

2 cups (475ml) heavy cream

¾ cup (150g) sugar

4 egg yolks

3 ounces (85g) dark chocolate (70% cacao), chopped into bits and chilled

This mint-basil chip ice cream is everything the green-hued mint chip of yesteryear isn't—in the best ways. It's lively, bright, floral, and, you know, tastes like mint. Whether your batch leans more toward basil or mint—or whether the two will be in perfect harmony—depends on the herbs you grab. Any which way, though, this ice cream will help you cope with a hard lesson: Giving up the groovy shade of green is worth it for flavor.

1. Warm the milk in a saucepan over medium-low heat. When gentle bubbles form on the edge, add the mint and basil. Off the heat, cover and let steep for 30 minutes or so.

2. Pass through a fine-mesh sieve into a small bowl, squeezing any remaining liquid out of the leaves. Return the milk to the saucepan along with 1 cup (240ml) of the heavy cream. Warm over medium heat.

3. Meanwhile, in a bowl, whisk together the sugar and egg yolks. Gradually whisk ½ cup (120ml) of the warm milk mixture into the egg yolks.

4. Pour the milk-yolk mixture into the saucepan, along with the remaining cup (235ml) of heavy cream.

5. Cook over medium heat 3 to 5 minutes, whisking all the while and being careful not to let it boil. When the base thickens enough to coat the back of a spoon, remove from the heat. Chill the base completely in the refrigerator for at least 4 hours but ideally overnight.

6. Pour the base into an ice cream maker and churn it according to the manufacturer's instructions. During the last minute of churning, add the chocolate.

Don't Be Bummed If Your Base Breaks

When you "break"—meaning overcook or curdle—your ice cream base on the stove, transfer it to a high-powered blender (or bring out the immersion blender). Blend until smooth, pass it through a fine-mesh sieve to get rid of the lumps, and continue with the recipe like nothing happened. The texture might not be exactly the same, but how much do you want to bet that no one notices?

Cinnamon Roll Ice Cream

Makes about 1 quart (950ml) | From Cristina Sciarra

Ice Cream

4 teaspoons cornstarch

2 cups (475ml) whole milk

1½ ounces (45g) cream cheese, at room temperature

⅛ teaspoon kosher salt

1¼ cups (300ml) heavy cream

⅓ cup (65g) granulated sugar

⅓ cup (75g) packed light brown sugar

¼ cup (20g) skim milk powder

2 tablespoons light corn syrup

1 tablespoon dark rum

2 teaspoons ground cinnamon

1 vanilla bean, split lengthwise

1 teaspoon vanilla extract

½ teaspoon active dry yeast

Swirl

4 ounces (115g) cream cheese, at room temperature

¼ cup (50g) light brown sugar

2 tablespoons solid coconut oil

2 teaspoons ground cinnamon

1 teaspoon vanilla extract

There are certain foods—pizza, tacos, bagels—too good to be contained to just one meal. Cinnamon rolls make that list, too. This ice cream has everything that is anything in the breakfast version: brown sugar, cream cheese icing reimagined as a cinnamon-laced swirl, and a good dose of vanilla. There's even yeast to get the pastry taste without sogginess. If you're still missing breakfast, though, make a pot of strong coffee, plunk a scoop of ice cream in—call it an affogato.

1. Whisk together the cornstarch and 2 tablespoons of the milk to make a smooth slurry. In a large bowl, whisk the cream cheese and salt until smooth.

2. In a 4-quart (3.8L) saucepan, whisk together the heavy cream, the remaining milk, both sugars, the milk powder, corn syrup, rum, and cinnamon. Add the vanilla seeds, pod, and extract. Bring to a rolling boil over medium-high heat and boil for exactly 4 minutes—the timing is critical. Off the heat, slowly whisk in the cornstarch slurry. Return the mixture to a boil over medium-high heat and cook, stirring constantly, until the mixture is slightly thickened, about 2 minutes. Off the heat, discard the vanilla bean pod.

3. Gradually whisk the hot milk mixture into the cream cheese. Pass through a fine-mesh sieve into a bowl. Chill completely for at least 4 hours but ideally overnight. When cold, stir in the yeast.

4. Pour the chilled base into an ice cream maker and churn it according to the manufacturer's instructions.

5. Meanwhile, to make the swirl, whisk together the cream cheese, brown sugar, coconut oil, cinnamon, and vanilla until smooth.

6. Spoon the ice cream into a container, layering it with spoonfuls of the swirl, and freeze.

Teatime Affogatos

Our COO, Bridget Williams, really likes affogatos—not with coffee, though, but rather Earl Grey tea poured over vanilla ice cream. Like any good exec, she encouraged us to innovate—what else could we affogato? Turns out, a lot! Rooibos tea and raspberry ice cream (page 63), matcha and basil-shiso gelato (page 89), mint tea and cucumber sherbet (page 140), English breakfast and apple–bay leaf ice cream (page 107), chamomile tea and cherry sorbet (page 92).

Dark Chocolate–Rosemary Ice Cream

Makes about 1 quart (950ml) | From Posie Harwood

1½ cups (355ml) whole milk

1½ cups (355ml) heavy cream

¾ cup (150g) sugar

¼ cup (10g) chopped fresh rosemary

¼ teaspoon kosher salt

1 vanilla bean, split lengthwise, or 1 teaspoon vanilla extract

¼ cup (20g) unsweetened cocoa powder

4 egg yolks

6 ounces (170g) dark chocolate (70% cacao), very finely chopped

Mint chocolate chip is the only ice cream flavor where you typically see chocolate hanging out with herbs, but reverse the proportions, switch up the herbs, and you have this, a sophisticated ice cream that's not at all uptight. It's deeply fudgy, complicated by piney rosemary, and best served with a glass of red wine or a cup of coffee. Use this infusion technique to bring other hard-stem herbs into your ice cream: thyme-orange, marjoram-strawberry, oregano–olive oil, and so forth.

1. In a large saucepan, whisk together the milk, cream, sugar, rosemary, salt, and vanilla bean seeds. Bring to a simmer over medium heat, stirring occasionally. Off the heat, cover and let steep for 30 minutes.

2. Pass the milk mixture through a fine-mesh sieve into a bowl, discard the rosemary, and pour back into the saucepan. Bring to a bare simmer over low heat, then off the heat, whisk in the cocoa powder until smooth.

3. In a small bowl, whisk together the egg yolks. Gradually whisk ½ cup (120ml) of the hot milk mixture into the yolks. Pour the milk-yolk mixture back into the saucepan and cook over medium heat until thick enough to coat the back of a spoon. Don't let it boil!

4. Off the heat, immediately stir in the chocolate until it melts.

5. Chill the ice cream base completely in the refrigerator for at least 4 hours but ideally overnight. Pour the chilled base into an ice cream maker and churn it according to the manufacturer's instructions.

Good, Old-Fashioned Hot Fudge (& Shake!)

Superuser Emily Connor loves a Dairy Queen shake, so, with inspiration from a *Gourmet* recipe, she set out to make her own. In a heavy saucepan over medium heat, stir to melt 3 ounces (85g) of finely chopped semisweet chocolate with ¼ cup (20g) unsweetened cocoa powder, ¼ cup (50g) packed dark brown sugar, ½ cup (120ml) golden syrup (preferably Lyle's), and ⅔ cup (160ml) heavy cream. Continue to cook at a low simmer for 5 minutes, stirring occasionally. Off the heat, add another 3 ounces (85g) of finely chopped semisweet chocolate, as well as 2 tablespoons unsalted butter cut into small pieces, 2 teaspoons vanilla, and a pinch of salt. Stir until smooth. Use the glossy, very chocolaty fudge on ice cream, or make it into a better-than-DQ shake with equal parts ice cream, milk, and hot fudge. Cooled sauce will keep in a covered container in the fridge for up to 1 week.

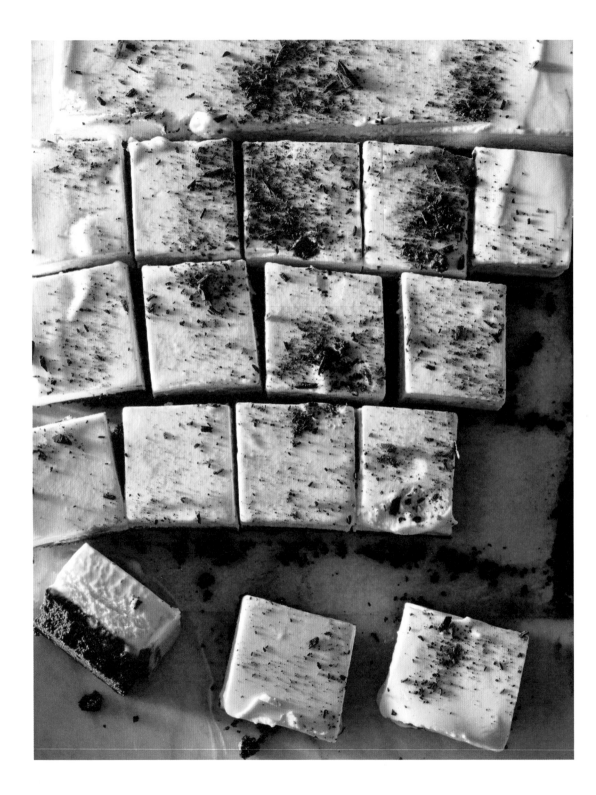

Grasshopper Ice Cream Bars

Makes 24 bars | From Cristina Sciarra

Crust

4 ½ cups (495g) chocolate cookie crumbs

½ cup (110g) coconut oil, melted

Fudge

3 ½ ounces (100g) dark chocolate (70% cacao), broken into pieces

2 tablespoons salted butter

¼ cup (20g) unsweetened cocoa powder

¼ cup (50g) granulated sugar

¼ cup (55g) packed light brown sugar

1 teaspoon cornstarch

1 cup (240ml) heavy cream

2 tablespoons light corn syrup

2 tablespoons crème de cacao

2 tablespoons crème de menthe

Grasshopper Ice Cream

1 (14-ounce/397g) can sweetened condensed milk

¼ cup (60ml) crème de menthe

This isn't a balloons-and-bounce-house ice cream cake. There's fudge, yes, but it's spiked—and the no-churn ice cream is also boozy from crème de menthe and crème de cacao. The other great news is there's added insurance against melt: It won't really start to soften until the 25-minute mark—just enough time to sing "Happy Birthday" and blow out some candles. For the chocolate cookie base, use your favorite chocolate shortbread recipe, Nilla chocolate wafers, or (our favorite) Effie's Cocoacakes.

1. To make the crust, evenly coat the cookie crumbs with coconut oil. Line a 9 by 13-inch (23 by 33cm) baking pan with parchment paper, leaving extra parchment hanging over the long sides of the pan.

2. Evenly press the cookie crumbs into the bottom of the pan and freeze until firm, about 30 minutes.

3. To make the fudge, simmer a pot with 2 inches (5cm) of water. Set a large, heatproof bowl with the chocolate and butter on top of the simmering water. Once the chocolate is melted, off the heat, whisk until smooth.

4. In a separate pot, whisk together the cocoa powder, both sugars, the cornstarch, heavy cream, corn syrup, crème de cacao, and crème de menthe. Cook over medium heat until simmering, whisking occasionally, until the mixture begins to thicken, about 15 minutes. Off the heat, whisk in the chocolate mixture. Let cool, about 30 minutes. (You can refrigerate the fudge in an airtight container for up to 2 weeks.)

5. Pour the cooled fudge over the crust and, using an offset spatula, spread it into an even layer. Freeze until the fudge is set, about 15 minutes.

6. To make the ice cream, stir together the condensed milk, crème de menthe, and crème de cacao in a large bowl.

7. Using a handheld electric mixer, beat the heavy cream on medium-high speed until stiff peaks form, 6 to 8 minutes.

CONTINUED

¼ cup (60ml) white crème de cacao (brown will muddy the green color)

2 cups (475ml) heavy cream, well chilled

Chocolate sprinkles, sauce, or shavings, for decorating

8. Mix a few spoonfuls of the whipped cream into the condensed milk mixture to lighten it. Add the remaining whipped cream and fold until fully incorporated. Don't overmix.

9. Spoon the ice cream over the fudge and smooth the top. Freeze for at least 5 hours but preferably overnight.

10. Lift the parchment paper to transfer the cake to a work surface. Decorate the top with chocolate sprinkles, swirls of chocolate sauce, or chocolate shavings. Cut the cake into 2-inch (5cm) squares and serve.

Carrot Cake Ice Cream

Makes a generous quart (950ml) | From Cristina Sciarra

Carrots

12 ounces (340g) carrots

3 tablespoons light brown sugar

2 tablespoons unsalted butter

1 teaspoon peeled, grated fresh ginger

1 teaspoon vanilla extract

1 teaspoon ground cinnamon

¼ teaspoon grated nutmeg

Rum Raisins

2 tablespoons dark rum

⅓ cup (50g) raisins

Candied Walnuts

¾ cup (75g) walnuts

1 tablespoon egg white

1 tablespoon light brown sugar

Ice Cream

1¼ cups (300ml) heavy cream

¾ cup (175ml) whole milk

¼ cup (20g) skim milk powder

½ cup plus 2 tablespoons (125g) granulated sugar

4 egg yolks

A carrot cake—even a great one—has many competing elements: strands of the namesake vegetable, then nuts, raisins, pineapple chunks, sometimes coconut, the occasional chocolate chip. And that's not even taking the swath of cream cheese icing into account. It's complicated to find your ideal cake—and in that cake, your ideal bite.

This ice cream quiets all that noise. With no dense, chock-full cake to fight against, the warm spices come to the foreground and the rum-soaked raisins and toasted walnuts can have presence. The cream cheese is incorporated into the base so that every bite has its tangy richness—no more competing with your loved ones for the most heavily frosted slice.

1. Coarsely chop the carrots. In a heavy saucepan, add all the ingredients for the carrots and ½ cup (120ml) water. Cook, covered, over medium heat, stirring occasionally, until the carrots are tender, about 20 minutes. Add more water as needed.

2. To make the raisins, bring a small pot with ½ cup (120ml) water and rum to a simmer over medium-low heat. Off the heat, add the raisins, cover, and let sit for 30 minutes. (The raisins can be refrigerated in their liquid for up to 3 days.) Drain the raisins, discarding the liquid.

3. To make the walnuts, heat the oven to 350°F (175°C). On a baking sheet, toss together the walnuts, egg white, and brown sugar. Bake until candied, about 10 minutes (watch them). Let cool, then coarsely chop. (They can be stored in a zip-top plastic bag at room temp for up to 2 days.)

4. To make the ice cream, whisk together the heavy cream, milk, milk powder, and ½ cup (100g) of the sugar in a pot. Bring to a simmer over medium-low heat, then remove from the heat.

5. In a separate bowl, whisk together the egg yolks with the remaining 2 tablespoons sugar for 30 seconds. Whisk the milk mixture into the yolks until incorporated.

6. Pour the milk-yolk mixture back into the pot and cook over medium-low heat, stirring occasionally, until the base thickens enough to coat the back of a spoon.

CONTINUED

1 cup (240ml)
mascarpone cheese,
at room temperature

4 ounces (115g)
cream cheese, at
room temperature

1 tablespoon dark rum

1 teaspoon vanilla extract

7. Add the carrots and their cooking liquid, mascarpone cheese, cream cheese, dark rum, and vanilla to the pot. Blend with an immersion blender until smooth, about 1 minute. Let steep for 30 minutes, then pass it through a fine-mesh sieve into a bowl. Chill the base completely in the refrigerator for at least 4 hours but ideally overnight.

8. Pour the chilled base into an ice cream maker and churn it according to the manufacturer's instructions. During the last 2 minutes of churning, add the raisins and walnuts.

What's Skim Milk Powder Doing in My Ice Cream?

Many ice creams have a good amount of milk (which is 90 percent water) and/or heavy cream (which is 60 percent water). So when the mixture goes into a frozen bowl and spins around, the water will freeze and you'll get ice cream; but if there's too much water, you'll get ice crystals, which will render your ice cream gritty. Enter skim milk powder, which absorbs the excess water that could be thwarting your best, creamiest intentions. Be sure to store milk powder in a cool, dry place, or the refrigerator. It is milk, after all.

Apple–Bay Leaf Ice Cream

Makes about 1½ quarts (1.4L) | From Cristina Sciarra

1 large apple, like Granny Smith, coarsely chopped

½ cup plus 3 tablespoons (140g) sugar

⅓ cup (80ml) unsweetened apple juice

2 cups (475ml) heavy cream

1 cup (240ml) whole milk

½ cup (35g) skim milk powder

4 egg yolks

1 dried bay leaf

For an ice cream that tastes like autumn on the most sweater-weather day, you want a crisp apple flavor. So let sweet roasted apples—and a bay leaf for earthiness—infuse your dairy-forward base. One bite and you'll get that feeling when you jump on fall leaves after eating too many apple-cider doughnuts.

1. Heat the oven to 425°F (220°C). In a small casserole dish, toss the apple pieces with 2 tablespoons of the sugar, then pour the apple juice over the apples. Roast until the juice is bubbling and the apple pieces are tender, about 25 minutes. Remove from the oven, then mash the pieces with a fork.

2. In a pot, whisk together the heavy cream, milk, milk powder, and ½ cup (100g) of the sugar. Bring to a simmer over medium-low heat, then remove from the heat.

3. In a bowl, whisk together the egg yolks with the remaining 1 tablespoon sugar for 1 minute. Gradually whisk the milk mixture into the yolks.

4. Pour the milk-yolk mixture back into the pot and cook over medium-low heat, stirring occasionally, until the ice cream base thickens enough to coat the back of a spoon.

5. Stir the apple mash and the bay leaf into the ice cream base. Let steep for 40 minutes, then pass it through a fine-mesh sieve into a bowl; discard the solids. Chill the base completely in the refrigerator for at least 4 hours but ideally overnight.

6. Pour the chilled base into an ice cream maker and churn it according to the manufacturer's instructions.

Genius Tip: Ice Cream Croutons

Bread can go in ice cream (page 148)—and on top, too. Brooks Headley, author of *Brooks Headley's Fancy Desserts*, uses toasted, lightly sweetened bread cubes as a crunchy counterpart to creamy gelato. Slit a loaf of bread down its middle, gut it of all the innards. Tear it into bite-size pieces and toss the pieces with sugar, a bit of salt, and olive oil. Bake at 350°F (175°C) until toasted, about 20 minutes, stirring halfway through. Use as a topping (or a bed!) for absolutely any ice cream.

Horchata Ice Cream

Makes about 1 quart (950ml) | From Cristina Sciarra

3 tablespoons long-grain
white rice

½ cup (70g) blanched
almonds

1 cinnamon stick

1½ cups (355ml)
heavy cream

¾ cup (150g) sugar

½ cup (35g) skim
milk powder

½ teaspoon ground
cinnamon

4 egg yolks

The first bite of this horchata-inspired ice cream will remind you of traditional *agua fresca*, the second will make you forget the other flavors, and, well, it won't take long for you to get to the last bite. Made in the traditional Mexican style—from rice, almonds, and cinnamon—it's everything we want between two snickerdoodles or after a taco *al pastor*—or anything, really.

1. Using a spice or coffee grinder, blitz the rice until it resembles a fine powder. In a bowl, stir together the rice powder, almonds, cinnamon stick, and 1½ cups (355ml) boiling water. Cover and let stand overnight.

2. Discard the cinnamon stick. Blend the rice mixture with 1 cup (240ml) cold water until smooth, 2 to 3 minutes. Strain the mixture through a nut-milk bag or a fine-mesh sieve lined with cheesecloth.

3. Pour 1½ cups (355ml) of the horchata into a pot (chill leftovers to drink). Add the heavy cream, ½ cup (100g) of the sugar, the milk powder, and cinnamon and cook over medium heat, whisking occasionally, until the sugar dissolves.

4. In a separate bowl, whisk together the egg yolks with the remaining ¼ cup (50g) sugar for 30 seconds. Gradually whisk the heavy cream mixture into the yolks.

5. Pour the cream-yolk mixture back into the pot and cook over medium-low heat, stirring occasionally, until the base thickens enough to coat the back of a spoon. Pass the base through a fine-mesh sieve into a bowl. Chill completely for at least 4 hours but ideally overnight.

6. Pour the chilled base into an ice cream maker and churn it according to the manufacturer's instructions.

The Anatomy of a Sundae

Despite common practice, throwing every sweet thing on top of ice cream is not going to get you a good sundae. Instead, practice restraint. For the sauce, consider chocolate sauce or ganache (page 14), caramel (page 85), butterscotch (page page 19), or jam. Your creamy topping might be whipped cream, marshmallow fluff, or meringue. And the extra-special toppings can be anything from sprinkles (page 4) to chopped and roasted nuts, fresh fruit, cereal, candy pieces, or chocolate chips. If you have sundae boats, you're probably already a pro at this sundae thing. For everyone else, get out a bowl or whiskey glasses. Start with an ice cream or two, then add sauce. Next the extra toppings, interspersed with the creamy topper. Then, go at it—unrestrained.

Drink Riffs

Thai Tea Snow Cone

Serves 10, generously | From Cristina Sciarra

1 cup (200g) sugar

5 bags Ceylon orange pekoe tea

2 star anise pods

2 green cardamom pods, crushed

2 cloves

2 teaspoons orange blossom water

1 (14-ounce/397g) can sweetened condensed milk

Restaurant Thai tea is usually brewed from a prepackaged mix of tea leaves, spices, and food coloring. This version, composed of ice instead of simply chilled by it, is more refreshing than sticky-sweet, with a strong tea taste and a list of spices you can customize (add vanilla; leave out the star anise; toss in a cinnamon stick!). For a nod to the original, spoon condensed milk over the top: It will pool in creamy pockets among the crunchy granita.

1. In a large saucepan, bring 8 cups (1.9L) water to a boil over high heat. When it's simmering, add the sugar and stir until dissolved. Once the water returns to a boil, remove from the heat. Add the tea bags, star anise, cardamom, cloves, and orange blossom water. Let steep for 45 minutes to 1 hour. Remove the tea bags and the aromatics. Refrigerate the tea until very cold, at least 3 hours or up to 3 days.

2. Pour the chilled tea into a wide casserole dish or baking pan. Freeze for 4 to 5 hours, scraping with a fork every hour or so, particularly around the edges, so the granita is broken into icy shards. (The granita will keep in the freezer for a couple weeks.)

3. When you're ready to serve, spoon some granita into glasses and drizzle 2 tablespoons sweetened condensed milk over the top of each.

Riff Away

Make an any-tea granita—mix 1 cup (240ml) freshly brewed and cooled tea (English breakfast, Earl Grey, green, herbal, you name it) with 3 tablespoons of superfine sugar dissolved in 2 tablespoons of freshly squeezed lemon juice. Pour it into a wide casserole dish or baking pan and freeze as directed. Alice Medrich suggests substituting finely ground French roast coffee beans for the Thai tea leaves and shortening the steeping time to 5 minutes. Top with condensed milk and you've got Vietnamese coffee granita.

Vanilla Rooibos Gelato

Makes about 1 quart (950ml) | From Cristina Sciarra

2 cups (475ml)
whole milk

1 cup (240ml)
heavy cream

¼ cup (20g) skim
milk powder

½ cup plus 1 tablespoon
(110g) sugar

1½ tablespoons light
corn syrup

5 egg yolks

1 tablespoon
vanilla extract

⅓ cup (30g) loose-leaf
vanilla rooibos tea or the
leaves from 15 tea bags

Compared with traditional American ice cream, gelato is lower in butterfat (4 to 9 percent as opposed to 14 to 25 percent), and when made commercially, it's churned at a lower speed, introducing less air into the mixture. So what does all of this mean for you? A creamier, denser, and softer dessert, with a silky elasticity that resembles marshmallow frosting. It's the ideal canvas for delicate red rooibos, a tea that comes from the leaves of a brushy plant native to southern Africa.

Because rooibos tea is sweetly earthy (similar to red bean and sweet potato) as well as floral (without being soapy—closer to honey than lavender), it's exciting on its own, and perhaps an even better pairing for a piece of fruit pie than classic vanilla.

1. In a pot, whisk together the milk, heavy cream, milk powder, ½ cup (100g) of the sugar, and the corn syrup. Bring the mixture to a simmer over medium-low heat, then remove from the heat.

2. In a small bowl, whisk together the egg yolks with the remaining 1 tablespoon sugar for 30 seconds. Gradually whisk the milk mixture into the yolks.

3. Pour the milk-yolk mixture back into the pot and cook over medium-low heat, stirring occasionally, until the base thickens enough to coat the back of a spoon.

4. Stir in the vanilla and the tea leaves. Let the warm base steep for 40 minutes, then pass it through a fine-mesh sieve into a bowl. Chill the base completely for at least 4 hours but ideally overnight.

5. If you have a gelato paddle, fit it on your ice cream maker. If you don't, don't worry about it! Pour the chilled base into the ice cream maker and churn it according to the manufacturer's instructions.

Coffee Frozen Custard

Makes about a quart (950ml) | From Cristina Sciarra

1¼ cups (300ml)
heavy cream

¾ cup (175ml)
whole milk

¼ cup (20g) skim
milk powder

6 tablespoons (75g)
sugar

3 tablespoons light
corn syrup

6 egg yolks

1½ tablespoons
espresso powder

1 teaspoon vanilla extract

Frozen custard should be thick yet soft—the epitome of luscious —and served right from the ice cream maker so its temperature and consistency resemble gelato. Let this coffee frozen custard (reminiscent of a really creamy frappuccino) firm up in the freezer and it'll be like the familiar coffee ice cream, but why trot into known territory? We encourage topping with dark chocolate shards, or chocolate-covered pretzels (page 23) or espresso beans.

1. In a pot, whisk together the heavy cream, milk, milk powder, ¼ cup (50g) of the sugar, and the corn syrup. Bring to a simmer over medium-low heat, then remove from the heat.

2. In a bowl, whisk together the egg yolks with the remaining 2 tablespoons sugar for 1 minute. Gradually whisk the cream mixture into the yolks.

3. Pour the mixture back into the pot and cook over medium-low heat, stirring occasionally, until the base thickens enough to coat the back of a spoon.

4. Add the espresso powder and the vanilla and let steep for 30 minutes, then pass the base through a fine-mesh sieve into a bowl. Chill the base completely for at least 5 hours but ideally overnight.

5. Pour the chilled base into an ice cream maker and churn it according to the manufacturer's instructions.

6. Serve straight from the machine for a true frozen custard experience, or spoon into a container and freeze for up to 2 hours before scooping. (Any longer and it will have more of an ice cream consistency.)

Genius Tip: Make It a Mocha, and Therefore Breakfast

Here's how to eat ice cream for breakfast. David Lebovitz suggests blending chocolate ice cream with a few shots of espresso for the most delicious mocha. Or do as they do in Australia: Top hot or chilled espresso with lots of ice and a scoop of vanilla ice cream (and maybe a bit of milk). Stir and top with whipped cream.

Earl Grey Ice Cream with Blackberry Swirl

Makes about 1 quart (950ml) | From Elina Cohen

1½ ounces (45g) cream cheese, at room temperature

⅛ teaspoon sea salt

1 tablespoon plus 1 teaspoon cornstarch

2 cups (475ml) 2% milk

1¼ cups (300ml) heavy cream

½ cup (100g) sugar

1½ tablespoons light corn syrup

2 tablespoons high-quality loose-leaf Earl Grey tea

1 tablespoon vodka

¼ cup (80g) blackberry jam, plus more as needed

Elegant and perfumy from loose Earl Grey tea leaves, every bite of this ice cream is citrusy with bergamot—and way more fun than high tea. Generous swirls of blackberry jam guard against primness and cut any of the tea's bitterness. Because the recipe uses jam instead of fresh berries, it can be made in any season—and easily modified if fig, plum, orange, or sour cherry is more your . . . jam.

1. In a bowl, mash the cream cheese and salt with a fork. In a small bowl, whisk together the cornstarch and 2 tablespoons of the milk.

2. In a large pot, bring the remaining milk, the heavy cream, sugar, and corn syrup to a simmer over medium heat. Continue to simmer, stirring constantly, for 4 minutes and no more. Off the heat, stir in the cornstarch slurry and return to a boil for another minute, stirring constantly until the mixture slightly thickens. Add the loose-leaf tea and let steep for 5 minutes. Don't be tempted to put the tea in a cheesecloth—you'll get a lot more flavor without one.

3. Add ¼ cup (60ml) of the hot milk mixture to the cream cheese, whisking well to break up any lumps. Then, whisk in the remaining hot milk mixture.

4. Chill the base completely in the refrigerator for at least 4 hours but ideally overnight.

5. Pass the ice cream base through a fine-mesh sieve into a medium bowl, pressing on the tea leaves. Stir in the vodka.

6. Pour the base into the ice cream maker and churn it according to the manufacturer's instructions.

7. Line a lidded glass container (like a loaf pan or a shallow rectangular pan) with plastic wrap, leaving extra plastic hanging over the edges. Spoon the ice cream into the container and drizzle thin streaks of jam. Spoon in more ice cream, layering it with more streaks of jam. Cover the ice cream with the overhanging plastic, close the container, and freeze.

8. Let the ice cream soften a couple of minutes before scooping. Create swirly scoops by pulling your ice cream scoop through (instead of along) the jam streaks.

Mud Pie with Beer Ice Cream

Serves 8 to 10 | From Cristina Sciarra

Pie Crust

10 ounces (280g) chocolate cookies (such as Nilla chocolate wafers or shortbread)

2 tablespoons confectioners' sugar

1 tablespoon all-purpose flour

1 tablespoon espresso powder

¼ teaspoon kosher salt

¼ cup (60g) unsalted butter, melted

3 teaspoons coconut oil, melted

3½ ounces (100g) dark chocolate (70% cacao), chopped

Whipped Cream

3 tablespoons unsweetened cocoa powder

2 tablespoons granulated sugar

1½ cups (355ml) heavy cream, well chilled

There's *Mississippi* mud pie: a chocolate wafer crust topped with a layer of chocolate pudding, cake, or both—and whipped cream. And then there's *mud pie* mud pie, where the crust is filled with coffee-flavored ice cream and drizzled with fudge. It's said to have been invented in 1957 by San Francisco restaurateur Joanna Droeger, who was mesmerized by a story that newlyweds Barbra Streisand and Elliott Gould kept a freezer under their bed so they could eat coffee ice cream without leaving their room.

This version has hints of both original desserts, but it's in a league all its own. The middle layer is made with lambic framboise, a Belgian, slightly sour raspberry beer that makes the ice cream so fluffy, you might think you're eating a frozen cream pie. And you can still eat the whole tall-and-mighty pie in bed, just like Barbra.

1. To make the pie crust, heat the oven to 350°F (175°C). Place a deep-dish, 9-inch (23cm) pie plate nearby.

2. Process the cookies in a food processor until reduced to fine crumbs, about 30 seconds. Add the confectioners' sugar, flour, espresso powder, and salt and pulse to combine. With the processor running, slowly pour in the melted butter and 2 teaspoons of the coconut oil and process until combined, about 30 seconds. Evenly press the crust into the bottom and sides of the pie plate. Bake until the bottom is firm, about 25 minutes. Let cool for at least 30 minutes.

3. Meanwhile, bring a pot with 1½ inches (4cm) of water to a simmer. Set a large, heatproof bowl with the remaining 1 teaspoon coconut oil and the chocolate on top of the simmering water until the chocolate melts. Off the heat, whisk together the coconut oil and chocolate until smooth. When the pie crust is cool, drizzle the melted chocolate all over the bottom and sides. Let cool for at least 1 hour.

4. To make the whipped cream, in a large bowl, combine the cocoa powder and granulated sugar. Whisk in ¼ cup (60ml) of the heavy cream. When the cocoa powder and sugar are dissolved, add the remaining 1¼ cups (295ml) heavy cream. Beat on medium-high speed until soft peaks form, about 2 minutes. Refrigerate while you make the ice cream and up to 1 day.

CONTINUED

Beer Ice Cream

1 (750ml) bottle
Lindemans
Framboise beer

1 (14-ounce/397g)
can sweetened
condensed milk

1 tablespoon
unsweetened cocoa
powder

2 cups (475ml) heavy
cream, well chilled

2 ounces (55g) dark
chocolate (70% cacao)
or cocoa nibs, for garnish

5. To make the ice cream, bring the beer to a boil in a wide saucepan over medium-high heat. Boil until the beer is reduced to just ½ cup (120ml), about 40 minutes. (The beer syrup can be refrigerated for up to 1 day.)

6. Pour the condensed milk into a large bowl. Stir in the beer syrup and the cocoa powder.

7. Pour the heavy cream into another large bowl and beat on medium-high speed until stiff peaks form, 6 to 8 minutes.

8. Mix a few spoonfuls of the whipped cream into the condensed milk mixture. Fold in the remaining whipped cream. Don't overmix.

9. Spoon the ice cream into the pie crust and smooth the top. Cover the ice cream with plastic wrap and freeze at least 3 hours, or up to 2 days.

10. Just before serving, spoon the chocolate whipped cream on top of the frozen beer ice cream. You can use a large spoon and make clouds, or put the whipped cream into a pastry bag and pipe swirls. To garnish, shave the chocolate with a vegetable peeler or sprinkle with cocoa nibs. Cut into wedges and serve.

Genius Tip: Slice Frozen Desserts with Ease

There's an unavoidable moment you have with every ice cream pie, cake, or bar you make: it's you and your knife against a veritable ice cube, melting imminent. Lucky for the integrity of your dessert and your stress level, Nicole Rucker, a Los Angeles pastry chef and blue ribbon–winning pie maker, offers a "hot" tip in *Lucky Peach*: "When you're ready to serve, soak a kitchen towel in very hot water and then unfold the towel so it lays flat. Place the pie on top of the towel—this prevents it from slipping and also releases the pie from the bottom of the frozen pie plate. Slice the pie with a hot, wet knife."

Rum Flambéed Banana Split

Serves 6 | From Cristina Sciarra

Banana-Caramel
Ice Cream

¾ cup plus 2 tablespoons (175g) granulated sugar

2 tablespoons salted butter

1¾ cups (415ml) heavy cream

1¼ cups (300ml) whole milk

½ cup (35g) skim milk powder

4 egg yolks

1 large, very ripe banana, chopped

1 tablespoon dark rum

1 teaspoon vanilla extract

Toasted Walnuts

½ cup (50g) walnuts

Whipped Cream

⅔ cup (160ml) heavy cream, well chilled

1 tablespoon granulated sugar

⅓ cup (80ml) mascarpone cheese

1 teaspoon vanilla extract

Bananas

¼ cup (60g) salted butter

¼ cup (55g) packed light brown sugar

1 vanilla bean, split lengthwise

6 firm bananas, sliced lengthwise

⅔ cup (160ml) dark rum

Banana splits always have a lot going on—many ice creams, whipped cream, chocolate syrup, maybe some berries, nuts, and a cherry on top. Oh, and banana too! It always gets forgotten. But keep the split's various components traveling in fewer directions and nothing gets pushed out of the boat. Here, the split is all banana (finally), rum, and cream.

The banana-caramel ice cream, mascarpone, flambéed bananas, and whipped cream all play well in other desserts, too. Top a cake with flambéed bananas, letting the sauce seep into the cake. Dollop any pie (or that banana flambé cake) with mascarpone whipped cream. Eat the ice cream whirred into a milkshake (page 32).

1. To make the ice cream, spread ¾ cup (150g) of the sugar in a wide, high-sided saucepan. Sprinkle 2 tablespoons water over the top and set the pan over medium-high heat. Cook for 5 minutes, watching it like a hawk, until it's light copper in color. Off the heat, whisk in the butter and ¼ cup (60ml) of the heavy cream. (Don't worry if there are lumps; you'll pass the base through a fine-mesh sieve.)

2. In a medium pot, whisk together the remaining 1½ cups (355ml) heavy cream, the milk, and milk powder. Bring the mixture to a simmer over medium-low heat, then remove from the heat.

3. In a bowl, whisk together the egg yolks with the remaining 2 tablespoons sugar for 1 minute. Slowly whisk in the milk mixture.

4. Pour the milk-yolk mixture back into the pot and cook over medium-low heat, stirring occasionally, until the base thickens enough to coat the back of a spoon.

5. Add the caramel, banana, rum, and vanilla. Puree with an immersion blender, 1 to 2 minutes. Let the base steep for 30 minutes, then pass it through a fine-mesh sieve into a bowl. Chill the base completely in the refrigerator for at least 4 hours but ideally overnight.

6. Pour the chilled base into an ice cream maker and churn it according to the manufacturer's instructions.

CONTINUED

7. Spoon the ice cream into a container and freeze. Makes about 1½ quarts (1.4L) of ice cream.

8. Prep the walnuts: Heat the oven to 350°F (175°C). Spread the walnuts across a baking sheet and bake until fragrant and toasted, about 10 minutes. Let the nuts cool, then coarsely chop. (The nuts can be stored in a zip-top plastic bag for up to 4 days.)

9. To make the whipped cream, in a bowl, beat the cream, sugar, mascarpone, and vanilla until soft peaks form, about 2 minutes. (The whipped cream can be refrigerated for up to 2 days.)

10. To make the bananas, in a wide skillet (do not use a high-sided pan), melt the butter and brown sugar. Add the vanilla bean seeds and pod. Stir over medium heat until the sugar dissolves, about 3 minutes. Add the bananas and cook for 3 to 4 minutes. Carefully flip them and cook the other side until browned and caramelized, 3 to 4 minutes more.

11. Off the heat, add the rum. Using a long match, light the rum on fire. (If you need to put out the flame, cover the pan with the lid.)

12. To serve, let the ice cream soften for 10 to 15 minutes. You can serve it family style, with everything heaped in the skillet with the bananas, or compose individual servings: Add a scoop of ice cream to a bowl, and nestle two banana halves around. Drizzle with rum flambé sauce, dollop with whipped cream, and sprinkle with walnuts.

Blood Orange–Negroni Pops

Makes 10 pops | From Cristina Sciarra

⅓ cup (65g) sugar

2 cups (475ml) blood orange juice (from about 8 oranges)

¼ cup (60ml) gin

¼ cup (60ml) sweet vermouth

¼ cup (60ml) Campari

1 teaspoon grated orange zest

After drinking your first, or fiftieth, Negroni, you know you want more—more citrus, more bitter, more deep-hued allure. And the answer, sometimes, is not to order another but rather to mix it with blood orange juice and freeze it into an ice pop (shown on page iv). Somehow it's more of a Negroni than the liquid version, more sultry in color, vivid in flavor, and still boozy. Rumor has it that eating three pops is the sweet—smiley, silly, not-sloppy—spot.

1. In a large bowl (preferably with a pour spout), whisk together ¾ cup (175ml) water and sugar until the sugar dissolves. Whisk in the blood orange juice, gin, vermouth, Campari, and orange zest.

2. Divide the mixture evenly into pop molds. Freeze for at least 5 hours before serving.

Shake It Up

For a frozen Negroni Sbagliato (meaning "messed up," because it has sparkling wine instead of gin), serve your pop in a glass of Prosecco. Or dip your pop in a mixture of orange zest and sugar (zest of an orange to ¼ cup/50g sugar is a good place to start). If a granita is more your style and you like your drinks strong, increase the gin, vermouth, and Campari to ½ cup (120ml) each, decrease the blood orange juice to 1¼ cups (300ml), and freeze and scrape the mixture as directed on page 113.

Make Mine a Manhattan

Makes about 1 pint (950ml) | From Angela Brassinga

Cherries

1 cup (120g) packed dried cherries, chopped

½ cup (120ml) rye whiskey

½ cup (100g) sugar

Whiskey Ice Cream

8 egg yolks

1 cup (200g) sugar

3 cups (710ml) whole milk

1½ cups (355ml) heavy cream

1 tablespoon rye whiskey

This rum raisin redo unbuttons the dark, boozy collar of a classic Manhattan. It's a dairy-forward base with a gentle lashing of whiskey and cherries soaked in, yes, more whiskey. You won't need vermouth or bitters—because the garnish is really all you want from a Manhattan, isn't it? These cherries will serve this ice cream and your future sodas and sundaes well.

1. To make the cherries, simmer the cherries, whiskey, and sugar over medium-low heat until the cherries soften and the liquid reduces to a thin syrup, 7 to 8 minutes. Pour into a bowl, stir, and let cool.

2. To make the ice cream, in a large bowl, whisk together the egg yolks and sugar until combined.

3. In a large, heavy saucepan, bring the milk and heavy cream just to a simmer over medium heat. Gradually whisk the milk mixture into the yolk mixture. Return the milk-yolk mixture to the saucepan and cook over medium-low heat, stirring occasionally, until the ice cream base thickens, about 15 minutes (don't allow it to boil!).

4. Stir the whiskey into the base, then pass it through a fine-mesh sieve into a bowl. Chill the base completely in the refrigerator for at least 4 hours but ideally overnight.

5. Pour the base into an ice cream maker and churn it according to the manufacturer's instructions. During the last minute of churning, add the cherries.

How Cold? Ice-Cold

That ice cream canister? It has to be frozen, like in-the-freezer-for-24-hours-in-advance frozen. Your ice cream mixture should also be as cold as possible before churning—chilling overnight is ideal but not essential. A warm mixture will result in a longer churn for a less-smooth ice cream (no matter how cold your canister is). The caramel or jam you want to swirl in shouldn't be warm, either, or it will freeze up crunchy. Once you churn the ice cream, move it to the freezer quickly. Although, there is enough time to sneak one—only one!—spoonful.

Brown Derby Float with Grapefruit Frozen Yogurt

Serves 4 to 8 | From Cristina Sciarra

Grapefruit Frozen Yogurt

⅔ cup (160ml) grapefruit juice

1 tablespoon grated grapefruit zest

⅔ cup plus 2 tablespoons (160g) sugar

1½ cups (355ml) whole milk

4 teaspoons cornstarch

2 ounces (55g) cream cheese, at room temperature

½ cup (120ml) heavy cream

¼ cup (60ml) light corn syrup

1¼ cups (300ml) full-fat plain Greek yogurt

Punch

2 cups (475ml) grapefruit juice

½ cup (120ml) bourbon

½ cup (120ml) freshly squeezed lime juice

¼ cup (85g) honey

1 teaspoon lemon bitters

3 cups (710ml) grapefruit soda, chilled

This float takes the ingredients of a Brown Derby cocktail—a 1930s-era shake-up of grapefruit, bourbon, and honey—to a more spritzy, daytime-appropriate place: The grapefruit frozen yogurt inspired by a recipe from Jeni Britton Bauer is creamy enough to mellow the pucker of the bourbon-spiked, honey-kissed grapefruit punch, which isn't boozy enough to have you wilting in the afternoon heat.

1. To make the frozen yogurt, in a small pot, whisk the grapefruit juice with 1½ teaspoons of the grapefruit zest and 2 tablespoons of the sugar. Cook over high heat until thick and syrupy, 3 to 4 minutes. Pass through a fine-mesh sieve into a bowl.

2. In a small bowl, whisk together ¼ cup (60ml) of the milk and the cornstarch to make a smooth slurry. In a large bowl, vigorously whisk the cream cheese until smooth.

3. In a saucepan, whisk together the remaining 1¼ cups (300ml) milk, the heavy cream, the remaining ⅔ cup (135g) sugar, the corn syrup, and the remaining 1½ teaspoons grapefruit zest. Bring to a rolling boil over medium-high heat and boil for exactly 4 minutes—the timing is critical. Off the heat, slowly whisk in the cornstarch slurry. Return the mixture to a boil over medium-high heat and cook, stirring occasionally, until the mixture is slightly thickened, about 2 minutes.

4. Whisk the hot milk mixture into the cream cheese. Stir in the yogurt and the grapefruit syrup. Pass the base through a fine-mesh sieve into a medium bowl. Chill completely in the refrigerator at least 4 hours but ideally overnight.

5. Pour the chilled base into an ice cream maker and churn it according to the manufacturer's instructions. Spoon into a container and freeze. Makes almost a quart (950ml).

6. To make the punch, in a large bowl or pitcher, whisk together the grapefruit juice, bourbon, lime juice, honey, and lemon bitters.

7. Just before you are ready to serve, gingerly stir in the grapefruit soda. Divide the frozen yogurt, followed by the punch, among 4 to 8 glasses. If it's not as foamy as you'd like, add more soda. Serve with long spoons.

Après Party Granita

Makes about 2 cups (475ml) | From Alice Medrich (adapted from *Pure Dessert*)

1 cup (240ml) red and/or white wine or flat beer

3 tablespoons sugar

Sweetened whipped cream, for topping (optional)

As the simplest but also the best use for your beer and wine dregs, this granita asks you to dissolve sugar in water and alcohol—red or white wine or flat beer—before freezing the mixture and flaking it with a fork every so often. It will be as robust or delicate as whichever bottle you start with—and a safe space to blend whites or reds or bubblies and not tell anyone. In case you need reminding: red mixed with white makes rosé.

1. In a bowl, stir together the wine(s) or beer, 6 tablespoons (90ml) water, and sugar until the sugar dissolves.

2. Pour the mixture into a wide casserole dish or baking pan and freeze. When partially frozen, use a fork to scrape into shards and crystals. Freeze again until frozen completely. Scrape once more. (The granita will keep in the freezer for a couple weeks.)

3. Divide the granita equally among stemmed glasses, dolloped with whipped cream, if desired, and serve.

Rhubarb-Gin Sorbet with Rose Cream

Serves 8 | From Yossy Arefi

Sorbet

1 cup (200g) sugar

1 pound (450g) rhubarb, chopped

2 tablespoons freshly squeezed lime juice

2 tablespoons light corn syrup

2 tablespoons gin, plus more chilled gin for serving

Rose Cream

½ cup (120ml) heavy cream

2 teaspoons sugar

4 to 8 drops rose water

Floral from the rose water, woodsy from the gin, lively from lime, and a little puckery (and pale pink) thanks to rhubarb, all the components in this light-as-air sorbet work in sunshiny harmony to get you one big frog-leap closer to twirling in a springtime meadow. And you needn't even wait for it to defrost—it's soft like a pillow straight from the freezer.

1. To make the sorbet, dissolve the sugar in ½ cup (120ml) water over medium-high heat. Add the rhubarb and simmer until the rhubarb is very tender and beginning to fall apart, about 10 minutes.

2. Blend until smooth, then add the lime juice and corn syrup and pulse to combine. Chill completely in the refrigerator for at least 4 hours but ideally overnight. When the base is cold, stir in the gin.

3. Pour the base into an ice cream maker and churn it according to the manufacturer's instructions.

4. Spoon the sorbet into a container and freeze.

5. To make the rose cream, in a bowl, beat the cream on medium-high speed until soft peaks form, about 2 to 3 minutes. Fold in the sugar, followed by the rose water, one drop at a time, until you like how it tastes.

6. Scoop the sorbet into bowls and top with a few drops of chilled gin and a spoonful of whipped cream.

The Best Way to Store Ice Cream

The ideal home for handmade ice cream is a faraway land where the temperature always remains the same and where it doesn't come into contact with air. While we can't give ice cream everything it wants, we can make it comfortable so it doesn't ice us out. First, pack the ice cream in small, shallow, airtight containers. Even zip-top freezer-safe plastic bags work. If you're using a container with a lid, for added protection, cover ice cream with a layer of parchment or wax paper so icy formations will stay at bay. Then put your ice cream in the back, lower reaches of your freezer, where the cold fluctuates the least. Now comes the hard part: Try not to open the freezer too much. It's for a good cause.

Savory

Black Pepper Feta Ice Cream

Makes about 1 quart (950ml) | From Cristina Sciarra

6 ounces (170g) feta cheese, at room temperature

5 ounces (140g) cream cheese, at room temperature

¾ cup (175ml) whole milk

1 tablespoon freshly squeezed lemon juice

½ teaspoon freshly ground black pepper

1¼ cups (300ml) heavy cream

⅔ cup (135g) sugar

¼ cup (20g) skim milk powder

4 egg yolks

If you're more of a barely-sweets person, or an after-dinner cheese wedge kind of person, then this ice cream is for you! It's more milky than cheesy, with a briny spunk and a buttery golden tint to each scoop (that's the egg yolks talking). There's plenty of sweet—this is ice cream, after all!—with teeny-tiny notes of pepper perking it all up. You'll want to freshly grind the peppercorns as fine as possible so you don't get a startling crunch in an otherwise smooth, custardy spoonful. Include it on a cheese plate for dessert or on the menu between courses with watermelon or strawberries, beet ice milk (page 153)—or a balsamic, maybe butterscotch, sauce (page 19).

1. In a large bowl, combine the feta, cream cheese, ½ cup (120ml) of the milk, the lemon juice, and black pepper. Using an electric mixer, whip on medium speed until smooth and fluffy, about 2 minutes.

2. In a pot, whisk together the heavy cream, ⅓ cup (65g) of the sugar, the remaining ¼ cup (55ml) milk, and the milk powder. Bring the mixture to a simmer over medium-low heat, then remove from the heat.

3. In a separate bowl, whisk together the egg yolks with the remaining ⅓ cup (70g) sugar for 30 seconds. Gradually whisk the milk mixture into the yolks.

4. Pour the milk-yolk mixture back into the pot and cook over medium-low heat, stirring occasionally, until the base thickens enough to coat the back of a spoon.

5. Blend the base with the feta mixture until smooth, 1 minute. Let steep for 30 minutes, then pass it through a fine-mesh sieve into a bowl. Chill the base completely in the refrigerator for at least 4 hours but ideally overnight.

6. Pour the chilled base into an ice cream maker and churn it according to the manufacturer's instructions.

Cucumber Sherbet

Makes about a quart (950ml) | From Winnie Abramson

2 English cucumbers
(peeling optional),
coarsely chopped

²/₃ cup (225g) honey

¹/₃ cup (80ml) crème
fraîche

Juice of 2 limes

3 tablespoons vodka

We're going to say it: This sherbet is as cool as a cucumber. The sweet greenness of cucumbers is amplified by honey and a zip of lime juice, then smoothed out with crème fraîche (make it even smoother by passing the pureed mixture through a fine-mesh sieve before churning). The crème fraîche is also what makes this frozen dessert more of a sherbet than a granita—there's dairy, but still no eggs. To really show off the secret star, serve with an extra dollop of crème fraîche on top (and honeycomb, too, if you're a lily-gilder).

1. Combine all of the ingredients in a blender and process until smooth.

2. Pour the mixture into your ice cream maker and churn it according to the manufacturer's instructions, until granita-like.

3. Serve the sherbet straight from the machine, or spoon it into a container and freeze if you want it to be firmer.

Genius Tip: When the Melt Is Unmanageable

Sometimes you get caught lazing in the sunshine and forget about the ice cream very quickly melting into something you could never eat with a spoon. Don't rush the container to the freezer—the next time you dig in, it'll be unappealingly icy. Instead, Momofuku Milk Bar's Christina Tosi gives us permission to keep on doing nothing: Let the ice cream melt fully, then rechurn it (you'll need at least half a tub for it to work). This is also the key to fixing the flavor of an ice cream you may not love. If you're without an ice cream maker, make lemonade, by which we mean milkshakes (page 32)—just add less milk than you would with firm ice cream.

Summer Corn Semifreddo with Rosemary Shortbread Crust & Blueberry Compote

Serves 10 to 12 | From Sarah Simmons

Rosemary Shortbread

1 cup (125g) all-purpose flour

2½ teaspoons fresh rosemary leaves, coarsely chopped

½ teaspoon kosher salt

½ cup (110g) unsalted butter, at room temperature

⅓ cup (65g) sugar

Corn Semifreddo

2 ears corn, shucked

4 cups (950ml) heavy cream

¼ vanilla bean, split lengthwise

8 egg yolks, at room temperature

¾ cup (150g) sugar

½ teaspoon kosher salt

Blueberry Compote

4 cups (600g) blueberries

½ cup plus 3 tablespoons (140g) sugar

1 tablespoon freshly squeezed lemon juice

After having corn budino (an Italian custard) at New York's Locanda Verde and then seeing a recipe for one in a James Beard Foundation newsletter, Sarah started playing with the combo of corn and cream in dessert form. What she ended up with is a semifreddo cake that works from all angles of savory, sweet, and herby: a corn semifreddo (the kernel of the idea, if you will) on a rosemary crust with jammy blueberries over top. Sometimes, she'll swap the compote for caramel sauce to play on caramel corn. We don't care how it's served to us: As our art director said when she tried it one day before noon, "This one is really special."

1. To make the shortbread, heat the oven to 300°F (150°C). Combine the flour, rosemary, and salt in a bowl.

2. In a large bowl, beat the butter and sugar on medium-high speed until creamy. Fold in the flour mixture ¼ cup (30g) at a time. Gather the dough into a ball, cover in plastic wrap, and chill in the refrigerator for 30 minutes to 1 hour.

3. Roll the dough into a rectangle that's ½ inch (1.3cm) thick, and cut into rectangles that are about the same size.

4. Arrange the rectangles on an ungreased baking sheet. Bake the shortbread until lightly browned, about 30 minutes.

5. Transfer the shortbread to a wire rack to cool completely. (Store in an airtight container at room temperature for up to 1 week.)

6. To make the semifreddo, cut the kernels from the corn cobs, reserving the cobs. In a large saucepan, combine the kernels, cobs, heavy cream, and vanilla bean seeds and pod.

7. Bring to a rolling boil over medium heat, transfer to a large bowl, cover with plastic wrap, and chill for at least 12 hours, or up to 2 days.

CONTINUED

8. Bring a medium pot with 1½ inches (4cm) of water to a simmer. In a stainless-steel or glass bowl, whisk together the egg yolks, ½ cup (100g) of the sugar, and salt. Set the bowl on top of the simmering water, making sure the bottom of the bowl does not touch the water. Whisk until the egg mixture is pale, thick, and creamy, 10 to 15 minutes. Put the bowl into a larger bowl of ice water to cool completely.

9. Discard the cobs and vanilla pod from the heavy cream mixture. Beat the cream on medium-high speed until thick. Add the remaining ¼ cup (50g) sugar and beat until stiff peaks form, 5 to 7 minutes.

10. Mix a quarter of the whipped cream into the cooled custard. Gently fold the remaining whipped cream into the custard.

11. Line a 9 by 13-inch (23 by 33cm) baking pan with two pieces of parchment paper, leaving extra parchment hanging over the long sides of the pan. Break up the shortbread into coarse crumbs with a mallet or in the food processor.

12. Spoon the custard mixture into the prepared pan and sprinkle with the shortbread. Cover the top with the extra parchment. Freeze for at least 8 hours, or up to 3 days.

13. To make the compote, in a saucepan, combine 2 cups (300g) of the blueberries, the sugar, and lemon juice. Bring to a simmer over medium-high heat, stirring frequently, until the juices release, 8 to 10 minutes.

14. Increase the heat to high, bring the mixture to a boil, and cook, whisking frequently, until the compote thickens, about 2 minutes. Transfer the compote to a bowl and gently fold in the remaining 2 cups (300g) uncooked berries.

15. Let the semifreddo sit at room temperature for 5 minutes. Line a large baking sheet with parchment paper.

16. Gently loosen the parchment and invert the pan onto the prepared baking sheet, lifting the pan and unmolding the semifreddo. Remove the parchment from the top of the semifreddo. Cut into squares, plate, and top with the blueberry compote.

Tomato Peach Basil Sorbet

Makes about 1½ quarts (1.4L) | From Cristina Sciarra

⅔ cup (135g) sugar

½ cup (10g) fresh basil leaves

2 pounds (900g) tomatoes (about 2 or 3 large)

1 pound (450g) peaches (about 2)

Three of summer's sweethearts and little else (no milk, cream, or even much sugar) blend together for this season-screaming, not-too-sweet dessert. Yes, it's one of those times that perfectly ripe produce is essential. You'll know why when you taste it.

1. In a pot, whisk 1 cup (240ml) water and sugar over medium heat until the sugar dissolves. Add the basil and let steep for 10 minutes. Strain the syrup through a fine-mesh sieve, pressing with the back of a spoon to extract all the liquid. (You can refrigerate the syrup in an airtight container for up to 3 days.)

2. Stem and halve the tomatoes. Use a spoon or your fingers to pull out the seeds; discard. Grate the tomato using the large holes of a box grater; discard the skins. Use a knife to peel and halve the peaches, remove and discard the pits, and coarsely chop the flesh.

3. Blend the basil syrup, tomato, and peaches until very smooth, about 1 minute. Strain through a fine-mesh sieve. Chill completely in the refrigerator for at least 2 hours but ideally overnight.

4. Pour the chilled base into an ice cream maker and churn it according to the manufacturer's instructions. It's best eaten right after churning, slightly slushy. If you do freeze it, take it out to soften for 15 minutes before scooping.

Genius Tip: Any-Berry, No-Cook Sorbet

Ruth Rogers and Rose Gray of The River Café have a secret for a more interesting, less sugary, crazy simple strawberry sorbet: lemon pith. Not only does it add depth to the otherwise sweet recipe, but it breaks down the sugar so that no simple syrup is necessary. It all happens in the food processor: Pulse a chopped lemon (we'll repeat: the whole lemon, coarsely chopped—just leave out the seeds if you can) with 2 cups (400g) sugar in a food processor. Transfer the lemon mixture to a bowl—don't bother cleaning the food processor. Puree 2 pounds (900g) strawberries in the food processor. Because we can't get enough of this recipe, we tried it with other berries—and even frozen ones—with smashing success. Add the pureed berries to the lemon mixture, along with the juice of a second lemon. Taste and add more juice if you want. Churn in the ice cream maker until frozen.

Burnt Toast Ice Cream

Makes about 1¼ quarts (1.2L) | From Cristina Sciarra

2 (¼-inch/6mm) slices country-style white bread

1¾ cups (415ml) heavy cream

1¼ cups (300ml) whole milk

½ cup plus 2 tablespoons (125g) sugar

½ cup (35g) skim milk powder

4 egg yolks

If burning toast is something you've been avoiding since the first time you used a toaster, think about how much you like toast and butter. Then consider that "burning" is pretty much the same thing as caramelizing, which is a really good flavor to have in an ice cream. Now take our word when we tell you that putting burnt toast bits in an ice cream makes it—there's no better word for it—*toasty*. It's the slightest bit savory, buttery from the cream, and flecked with fine toast crumbs or "dust," as Cristina calls it. Plus, think of how devilish you'll feel burning the heck out of toast *on purpose*.

1. Toast the bread long enough to develop a deep brown color, even black in spots. Blitz the toast to dust in a food processor.

2. In a pot, whisk together the cream, milk, ½ cup (100g) of the sugar, and the milk powder. Bring to a simmer over medium-low heat, then remove from the heat.

3. In a bowl, whisk together the egg yolks with the remaining 2 tablespoons sugar for 1 minute. Gradually whisk the milk mixture into the yolks.

4. Pour the milk-yolk mixture back into the pot and cook over medium-low heat, stirring occasionally, until the base thickens enough to coat the back of a spoon.

5. Add ¼ cup (25g) of the burnt toast dust to the ice cream base (use any extra for garnish). Let the warm base steep for 30 minutes, then pass it through a fine-mesh sieve into a bowl. Chill the base completely in the refrigerator for at least 4 hours but ideally overnight.

6. Pour the chilled base into an ice cream maker and churn it according to the manufacturer's instructions.

Burnt Toast x Food52

Burnt toast isn't just special to us because it's an awesome ice cream flavor. Burnt Toast was the original name for our company. And years later, it became the name of our podcast!

Butternut Squash & Tahini Ice Cream with Caramelized Almonds

Makes about 1 quart (950ml) | From Posie Harwood

Ice Cream

1 (1½-pound/680g) butternut squash, peeled, seeded, and cut into 2-inch (5cm) cubes

1 tablespoon unsalted butter, cubed

2½ cups (590ml) whole milk

5 cinnamon sticks

¾ cup plus 3 tablespoons (185g) sugar

½ cup (120ml) heavy cream

½ cup (125g) tahini, stirred in the jar

¼ teaspoon kosher salt

5 egg yolks

Caramelized Almonds

¾ cup (70g) sliced almonds

3 tablespoons sugar

Pinch of kosher salt

Oh, is it squash for dinner? Roast off even more and you're a few steps closer to soup or salad and, more important, ice cream. When soothed by the heat of the oven, butternut squash can get sweet, so much so that earthy tahini gets called on to ground the flavors. What makes this a triple threat of an ice cream, though, is the caramelized almonds—they stay crunchy, they bring bites of caramelly sweetness, and they're probably really good in that salad you're making too.

1. To make the ice cream, heat the oven to 375°F (190°C). Put the squash on a foil-lined baking sheet and dot with the butter. Cover with more foil and roast until tender, about 45 minutes.

2. When the squash is cool enough to handle, puree in a blender or food processor until very smooth. Measure out 1½ cups (355ml) of the puree into a large bowl (save any remaining puree for dinner).

3. Bring the milk and cinnamon sticks to a boil over medium heat. Off the heat, cover and let sit for 30 minutes.

4. Pour 2 cups (475ml) of the cinnamon-infused milk into a separate saucepan. Stir in ½ cup (100g) of the sugar, the heavy cream, tahini, and salt and bring to a boil over medium-low heat.

5. Meanwhile, in a large bowl, whisk together the egg yolks and the remaining ¼ cup plus 3 tablespoons (85g) sugar. Once the milk mixture boils, gradually whisk it into the bowl of egg yolks and sugar. Cook over medium-low heat, whisking constantly, until thickened slightly, about 7 minutes. Pour the hot custard into the squash puree and whisk very well. Let cool to room temperature, then chill completely in the refrigerator overnight.

6. Pour the base into an ice cream maker and churn it according to the manufacturer's instructions.

7. Meanwhile, make the almonds. Cook the almonds, sugar, and salt in a saucepan over medium heat, stirring occasionally, until the sugar is dark amber and caramelized, about 10 minutes. Transfer to a plate and let cool.

8. Break up the almonds and add to the ice cream during the last minute of churning.

Beet Ice Milk

Makes a generous quart (950ml) | From Cristina Sciarra

1 pound (450g) beets, peeled and chopped

2 ½ cups (590ml) whole milk

¾ cup (150g) sugar

½ cup (120ml) heavy cream

¼ cup (20g) skim milk powder

1 tablespoon vodka

Without as much butterfat as ice cream, ice milk lets flavor ring through clear as a bell—and the texture, far from icy, is almost fluffy (like a good sorbet). So the ice milk is not shy in its beet-ness, simultaneously bright and rooty. As a result, it's good with all the ingredients beets themselves are good with: a scoop of any-berry, no-cook sorbet (page 147) or feta ice cream (page 139); curlicues of candied citrus peel (see below); or chocolate. Have you ever had beet-chocolate cake? It's good! Serve this ice milk with it, or half-melted over a warm brownie—and/or with chocolate shavings on top.

1. In a high-powered blender or food processor, puree the beets, ½ cup (120ml) water, and ½ cup (120ml) of the milk, about 2 minutes. Pour into a pot, then whisk in the remaining 2 cups (470ml) milk, the sugar, heavy cream, and milk powder. Bring to a simmer over medium-low heat. Off the heat, stir in the vodka.

2. Let the warm base steep for 30 minutes, then pass it through a fine-mesh sieve into a bowl. Use a spoon to gently push through the juice; discard the pulp. Chill the base completely in the refrigerator for at least 4 hours but ideally overnight.

3. Pour the chilled base into an ice cream maker and churn it according to the manufacturer's instructions. Spoon the ice milk into a container and freeze.

Make Candy out of Citrus Peels

To make candied citrus peels, peel the fruit (any citrus will work), then cut the peel into thin strips. Bring a saucepan with the peels and cold water to a boil, then keep the strips in there for a minute or two. This will help mellow the peels' texture and flavor—how long it cooks for really depends on the punchiness of the peel. Drain the peels into a bowl of cold water. If they still seem tough, blanch them again. In the same saucepan, bring a 1 to 1 ratio of water and sugar to a boil, stirring so the sugar dissolves. You'll need about a cup of each (250ml and 200g, respectively) for 3 lemons. Add the peels and turn the heat down to simmer for about 15 minutes, until the peels are bendy and shiny. Use a slotted spoon to transfer the peels to a wire rack over a lined baking sheet. Once dried, let the sweet-tart peels twirl atop ice cream: beet ice milk, lavender–coconut milk ice cream (page 88), or rhubarb-gin sorbet (page 134) to start.

Avocado Gelado

Makes about 1 quart (950ml) | From Abbie Argersinger

2 cups (475ml)
whole milk

1 vanilla bean, split
lengthwise

4 egg yolks

1 cup (200g) sugar

3 perfectly ripe avocados

Juice from 1½ lemons

1 cup (240ml)
heavy cream

The idea for this avocado gelado—that's "gelato" intentionally misspelled because rhyming is fun—came from an avocado shake at a Brazilian restaurant where Abbie once worked. And while this surprisingly creamy (thanks, avocado!) gelado is great on its own—and in a shake—the options for experimentation are many. To start, make a shake with two scoops of the gelado and great chocolate milk. Then, try using lime juice instead of lemon or mixing in chocolate chips (page 8) during the last minute of churning. Drizzle over hot fudge (page 99) for an avocado sundae. Add some broiled citrus (see below) to your bowl. Right about now, your avocado toast is starting to look just a little boring, isn't it?

1. In a saucepan, bring the milk and vanilla bean seeds and pod to a simmer over medium-low heat, then remove from the heat and let steep for about 30 minutes.

2. Whisk in the egg yolks and sugar, then bring it back to a simmer over medium-low heat, whisking constantly, until a thick custard forms. Let cool again, then refrigerate the custard for at least 2 hours but ideally overnight.

3. Chop the avocado into cubes, then blend with the lemon juice and heavy cream. Discard the vanilla bean pod. Add the custard to the avocado mixture and blend until smooth.

4. Pour the base into an ice cream maker and churn it according to the manufacturer's instructions.

Scorched, Sweet Citrus

If old-fashioned broiled grapefruit put on a little black dress, they'd look like this: slinky slices glazed with burnished sugar. To make broiled citrus slices, heat the broiler and position the rack 4 to 5 inches (10 to 13cm) from the heat. Cut the top and bottom off of any citrus and stand it up on one of the flat sides. Run your knife from the northern to southern hemisphere between the fruit and the pith to get rid of the peel and pith. Cut the citrus lengthwise into ½-inch (1.3cm) slices. Place the slices on a parchment-lined baking sheet and sprinkle with a thin layer of turbinado sugar. Broil so the sugar is deeply caramelized and edges start to blacken. Serve atop or below ice cream.

Thank Yous

Ice cream is a whole lot more fun with friends, and writing a book is, too.

This book would have in no way been possible without Food52's community members who dared to dream creamier, kookier, and bigger with their ice creams. Thank you for sharing your recipes and wisdom with all of us at Food52 and now in this book. Our freezer is a lot more fun and exciting because of each of you: Abbie Argersinger, Alice Medrich, Amanda Hesser, Angela Brassinga, Barbara Reiss, Big Gay Ice Cream, Bobbi Lin, Brooks Headley, Christina Tosi, Cristina Sciarra, Cynthia Chen McTeman, David Lebovitz, Derek Laughren, Elina Cohen, Emiko Davies, Emily Connor, Emily Vikre, Ethan Frisch, Kathy Wielech Patterson, Katie Quinn, Lisa Canducci Bailey, Liz Larkin, Mandy Lee, Marian Bull, Mary French, Max Falkowitz, Merrill Stubbs, Michelle Lopez, Molly Yeh, Mrs. Mehitabel, Nicholas Day, Nicole Rucker, Pat Aresty, Phyllis Grant, Posie Harwood, The River Café, Sarah Simmons, Suzanne DeBrango, Virginia Kellner, Winnie Abramson, and Yossy Arefi. A special thank-you to Alice Medrich, who has flooded our website with invaluable information about ice cream and was there to answer phone calls and give advice on probably unnecessary worries.

Thank you to Cristina Sciarra, our ice cream sherpa who leaves no flavor or serving idea unconsidered, but doesn't flinch when we suggest another (burnt toast) and then another another (lemon spoom?). We can't pick our favorite of the 30 recipes you developed for this book, so we won't! Thank you for lugging your industrial ice cream maker from Jersey for shoots, and for responding to e-mails in record time.

The editors—Kristen Miglore, Ali Slagle, Sarah Jampel, Kenzi Wilbur, Amanda Sims, Caroline Lange, Samantha Weiss-Hills, and Leslie Stephens— ate ice cream before 10 a.m. and wrote headnotes that make each recipe sound like the special snowflake that it is. You are all also special snowflakes. This book wouldn't be what it is without Sarah, whose many (in a good way) ideas about how to make ice cream more fun made Ali's job of Frankensteining this book together a whole lot easier.

To the photo team, we did it! James Ransom and Alexis Anthony, thank you for loving our muse not just for how it tastes, but also for how it looks. Thank you to James for agreeing to shoot this book while on a Paleo diet, and to Alexis for finding yet another way to show a scoop of ice cream. Kristen and Sarah, ice cream styling is hard, but we found our way. Let's just not do it without air conditioning again, okay? Thank you to Josh Cohen and his helpers Allison Buford, Elizabeth Parlin, Scott Cavagnaro, Elena Apostolides, and Shannon Elliot for filling two freezers with ice cream, week after week—and for only kind of freaking out when our ice cream maker died.

Thank you to our testers—Anna Francese Gass, Dawne Marie Shonfield, Jennifer Philipp, Kate Knapp, Lauren Shockey, and Marisa Robertson-Textor—for facing brain freeze in the dead of winter and isolating the great from the good recipes. You're welcome for making you eat ice cream. Our gratitude to Head Recipe Tester, Stephanie Bourgeois, for answering e-mails with subject lines like "burnt toast dust measurement" without guffawing. Big thank you to CB Owens, too, for your attention to detail and caring about punctuation as much as we love ice cream.

To Amanda, Merrill, and the rest of the Food52 team, thank you for sharing our belief that ice cream knows no bounds in flavor, season, method, or joy; for participating in ice cream socials, often; and for doing all the behind-the-scenes stuff you do to bring this book to life.

Ten Speed: We know that each of you has touched this book in some way. Thank you for your belief in a different, looser, sillier ice cream book, and for helping us make one—that's just silly enough.

Index

Published in the United States by Ten Speed Press, an
imprint of the Crown Publishing Group, a division of
Penguin Random House LLC, New York.
www.crownpublishing.com
www.tenspeed.com

Ten Speed Press and the Ten Speed Press colophon are
registered trademarks of Penguin Random House LLC.

Library of Congress Cataloging-in-Publication Data is
on file with the publisher.

Hardcover ISBN: 978-0-399-57802-1
eBook ISBN: 978-0-399-57803-8

Printed in China

Design by Margaux Keres

10 9 8 7 6 5 4 3 2 1

First Edition